The Art of JOHN DRYDEN

SOUTH ATLANTIC MODERN LANGUAGE
ASSOCIATION AWARD STUDY

The Art of
JOHN DRYDEN
by Paul Ramsey

UNIVERSITY OF KENTUCKY PRESS

LEXINGTON *1969*

This book is dedicated to

GEORGE M. KAHRL

in respect and friendship

Contents

Acknowledgments

In 1956 I finished a thesis on John Dryden at the University of Minnesota under the kind and brilliant tutelage of Samuel Holt Monk. My gratitude and friendship to him have continued and grown. The germ of this book was in the thesis, and there is overlap, but the great majority of the thesis is omitted. Most of this book has been written in the last five years.

My other debts are many. Specifically, I wish to thank the University of the South and the University of Chattanooga (now the University of Tennessee at Chattanooga) for research grants, and, for many courtesies, the librarians and staffs of several libraries including those of the University of the South, the University of Chattanooga, Emory University, and the University of California at Berkeley; the Joint University Libraries at Nashville; the Library of Congress; the British Museum; and the Folger Shakespeare Library. Two members of the Folger staff have given me special and highly competent assistance, Miss Anne Wadsworth in verifying references and Miss Sylvia Fleming in indexing. Mrs. Ray Pradat, Miss Hilda Frazier, and Miss Mary Dacey have each typed a share of a much revised and sometimes intricate manuscript with patience and cheerfulness as well as high skill. Dr. Harold F. Brooks of Birkbeck College of London University read the manuscript and made a number of excellent suggestions, some of which I have had the wit to follow.

The debt of this book to the excellent modern scholarship on Dryden and related subjects is visible throughout in text and notes. Two somewhat earlier writers deserve at least a word. George Saintsbury is so much rebuked by scholars these days that I tremble a little at my temerity in offering a word of praise. His faults were real enough, but so were his virtues. One of his chief virtues, for me an overweighing one, is that he did respond to the rhythmical reality of poems. The one secondary source that has probably had the greatest impact on my thinking and feeling about Dryden's poetry is A. W. Verrall's *Lectures on Dryden,* an exciting and somewhat neglected book. I am glad to see that it has been reissued.

My personal and professional debt to the distinguished scholar to whom the book is dedicated is very great; it gives me joy to acknowledge it.

1

The Faire Designment: Dryden on Verse and Design

JOHN DRYDEN is a critic more than a theorist. He judges poetry thoughtfully; he talks incomparably well about it. But he also likes to think and to speak of his thinking, to explore and mediate literary principle, to blend inference with metaphor, to seek loadstone and pole star,[1] then to set his course as his judgment (or fancy) allows. He wrote with ease and at times carelessly, but he knew where he stood.

His view of criticism and poetry is theistic: he knows that nature is intelligible, and therefore that poetry and criticism can be. The world is created, its value real. But it is a great and puzzling world, "so almost infinite and boundless as can never fully be comprehended but where the images of all things are always present."[2] Theory misses something in nature; but to deny intelligibility is

1

to destroy art. Dryden seeks order, not formula; vitality, not chaos.

Nature is felt to be a personification of itself, a life-giving power that derives from the ordered, vigorous whole of the universe. At the same time, nature is not in one sense all-inclusive: the unnatural and the chaotic always threaten us; wisdom, order, principles are necessary to constrain them. In esthetics as in ethics, nature is at once a metaphysical reality and a moral-esthetic order, in which Dryden, consciously and at the deepest levels of assumption, strongly believed. That inherited ontological faith has great value to him as a critic and as a poet. It is less "thinly diluted" than has been thought.[3] Nature to Dryden is not vague;[4] it is rich with meaning and variety. It is not mechanical;[5] it is instinct with life. It is not uniformitarian;[6] it is hierarchical and allows for individuality. Nature is not a mere lexical multiplicity;[7] it is a reality. It is, under God, *the* reality. Since God transcends man, God's world is mysterious to us; since God creates intelligibly, there is much for us to understand.

Poetry is an image of nature. An image is an artifact, a thing in itself, as well as a representation of something outside itself. Dryden's view of poetry leaves room for poetry as invention and for man's imagination, for the mind is natural too.

The crucial truth about Dryden's criticism is that it is consistent in fundamentals (literature stands on the "great foundation"[8] of nature: it should be a just and lively and proper image of nature for the delight and instruction of mankind,[9] because the spirit of man cannot be satisfied but with truth or at least verisimility),[10] yet flexible in dealing with secondary principles and in assigning priorities between modern and ancient, fancy and judgment, nature and art, instruction and delight. Dryden distinguished between the primary, unshakable rules and the secondary rules which require mediation and qualification.[11] To be sure, not all his inconsistencies reduce to dialectical balancings and shadings, though many do. The all-but-standard view of Dryden as inconsistent holds some truth, since he is tentative and unremembering, lively at addressing the issue at hand; but that is a subsidiary truth, a failure in him (as to no little degree in all great critics) to order perfectly his riches. He worked within a largely sound and developing tradition.[12] Within it, he walked at large.

He sometimes applies his general convictions too schematically, or too carelessly, or too glibly. But he usually has a nice sense of the respect due to theory and experience. In that he is centrally right; he knew instinctively and by theory what many critics and literary theorists never learn: that theory tends to enwind itself, to breed aridities; yet caprice is at last caprice. Before I turn to his specific beliefs about design and versification, I would like to look at one application of his general theory, one that shows some central features of his beliefs and methods. The passage is from "The Author's Apology for Heroic Poetry and Poetic Licence," his preface to *The State of Innocence.*

> Thus I grant you that the knowledge of nature was the original rule; and that all poets ought to study her, as well as Aristotle and Horace, her interpreters. But then this also undeniably follows, that those things which delight all ages must have been an imitation of nature; which is all I contend. Therefore is rhetoric made an art; therefore the names of so many tropes

and figures were invented: because it was observed that they had such and such effect upon the audience. Therefore catachreses and hyperboles have found their place amongst them; not that they were to be avoided, but to be used judiciously, and placed in poetry as heightenings and shadows are in painting, to make the figure bolder, and cause it to stand off to sight.

(Watson, I, *200–201*)

The appeal to authority and tradition is not a denial of nature or an appeal against the rules; it shows how the rules are grounded and limited. Men can go wrong, but they also can and should go right. They do go right when they follow their true nature, which is part of an intelligible, because created, world. This view is not a simplifying rationalism; Dryden is using it to justify under the proper conditions the apparently irrational devices of catachresis and hyperbole. He believes in reason as a valid instrument; he believes in a vigorous and intelligible nature even more fundamentally. What really delights must respond to the order of value (which is in the order of nature); therefore catachreses and hyperboles can be valuable. But hyperboles and catachreses are also in some ways clearly improper to truth (hyperboles are by definition not truth, catachreses violate normal rules for correct language), and therefore must be limited. Dryden escapes the contrary dangers of anarchy and narrowness by a metaphor.[13] He balances one partial truth against another (truths based on probable reasoning) to support what underlies each truth: the propriety of good style to the truth of nature and to permanent human psychology (itself part of nature).

This then is the bedrock of Dryden's criticism: to

image nature, there must be rules, since nature is intelligible. The articulation of these rules is an admirable but uncertain labor, since nature is also mysterious and our minds fallible: the detailed rules deserve real but not unqualified respect. The rules exist in order to effect a more just and lively image of human nature, through natural accords between subject, style, and audience. Since these accords exist, a dialectic between claims is possible. Propriety is a necessary concept, because those accords exist; it has no meaning without them. Dryden's view of propriety is sometimes seen as too narrow, inorganic, or merely decorative. But fundamentally it is anything but narrow; it is rooted in his deepest ontological awareness; and he applies the concept of propriety (a concept without which one cannot really judge poetry at all) in ways that are often mediative and beautifully imaginative.

Dryden's critical qualities are handsome ones, preferable to most. He has confidence in his basic assumptions; he moves gracefully within his traditions; he plays example against theory, theory against example; he mediates rival claims; his wit turns at various obliquities; he has his momentary enthusiasms and his genuine changes of mind. These qualities, which make for strength and flexibility as well as charm, also make it hard to sum his views, on design as on many other poetic topics. What he says about design has some unity of substance and some striking differences of claim.

Poems, he tells us, should be well designed; design has a high priority. A "view of the whole" is essential to good judgment.[14] Design is rooted in permanent human nature, affected only in nonessentials by the temporary and local, for "nothing can move our nature, but by

5

some natural reason, which works upon passions." [15]
Plot is one of the two "living Beauties of a Play" (wit
being the other). [16] Variety with unity is best, such a
variety that "the beauty of the whole be kept entire." [17]
Parts should "naturally" proceed from each other, both
in plays and in Pindarics. [18] In poems that catch the
"proper motions" of objects, we should see "the soul of
the poet . . . informing and moving through all his
pictures." [19]

Those views are true and necessary; they stand on the
great foundation. Something more particular and inconsistent appears in his ranking and analysis of design and
in his analogies for it.

How important is design in a work? Dryden says what
he pleases, and he pleases to say different things. Like
Aristotle, he sometimes thinks of design as separable
and abstract structure; unlike Aristotle, he does not
think of design as exclusively or primarily plot. In the
Preface to *Troilus and Cressida,* he does say that plot "is
the foundation of the play" and "that which is most
necessary," but goes on to say that "it strikes not the eye
so much as the beauties or imperfections of the manners, the thoughts, and the expressions," and shortly
thereafter says that the action is "built upon the moral"
(Watson, I, *247–48*). Thus, in one short passage of an
essay in which he is trying to state an accurate and
general theory, he gives (or seems to give) top ranking
to (1) the plot, (2) the manners, thoughts, and expression, (3) the moral.

In the 1668 Prologue to *Secret-Love* he seems to give
plot and wit (by *wit* I presume he here means his definition "a propriety of thoughts and words") [20] equal and
top ranking:

6

> He fears his Wit, or Plot he did not weigh,
> Which are the living Beauties of a Play.

In *An Essay of Dramatic Poesy*, he says that "the soul of Poesy" is "imitation of humour and passions" (Watson, I, 56), a view he supports elsewhere.[21] At least once, imaging becomes the most important element: "Imaging is, in itself, the very height and life of poetry."[22] In context he is evidently thinking of imagery as mainly expressive of character, though with an interesting hint that imaging also is structural in developing action: "If poetry be imitation, that part of it must needs be best which describes most lively our *actions* [emphasis mine] and passions; our virtues and our vices; our follies and our humours."

Such inconsistencies, if frustrating, express something of Dryden's genial spirit: what interests him at the moment is apt to seem to him the most important. Contrarily, what did not at the moment interest him is apt to seem to him unimportant, as in a passage in his Preface to *An Evening's Love* in which he shows something like contempt for plot:

> The story is the least part of either [the work of a poet and the graces of a poem]: I mean the foundation of it, before it is modelled by the art of him who writes it; who forms it with more care, by exposing only the beautiful parts of it to view, than a skilful lapidary sets a jewel. On this foundation of the story the characters are raised: and, since no story can afford characters enough for the variety of the English stage, it follows, that it is to be altered and enlarged with new persons, accidents, and designs, which will almost make it new. When this is done, the forming

7

it into acts and scenes, disposing of actions and passions into their proper places, and beautifying both
with description, similitudes, and propriety of language, is the principal employment of the poet. . . .

But in general, the employment of a poet is like that
of a curious gunsmith or watchmaker: the iron or
silver is not his own; but they are the least part of
that which gives the value; the price lies wholly in the
workmanship.

(Watson, I, *154–55*)

The "story" that is the "least part" is, to be sure, the
story as it exists before the playwright remakes it; the
plot in our sense is the story after the author has "mod-
elled" it. But in the passage Dryden does not betray
much interest in the story before or after; and "I mean"
has a ring of afterthought. The whole passage has a
distinct air of stasis, as do the metaphors of places,
silver, and workmanship. Any conceptualizing is apt to
tend to the static: spatial metaphors fit the analytic
mind more sedately than temporal ones. But Dryden's
interest here is not trained on the active as active, perhaps because Dryden himself realized that the plot of his
play was dull.

The "disposing of actions and passions" is a shade
obscure. How do those "actions" differ from the action
got, added to, then formed in the earlier part of the
sentence? He is perhaps misled by the neatness of the
rhetorical distinctions of *inventio, dispositio, elocutio,*
which his word "disposing" suggests he had in mind.[23]
Those only too neat distinctions he is apt to suggest,
here and elsewhere, are chronological as well as analytic. To be sure, when a playwright starts with an old
plot, he starts with it, and what he does to it must come

8

later in time, though not in so tidy an order as his statement suggests.

That division, the significantly ugly word "beautifying," and the image of the "curious gunsmith"—all suggest the view that language and thought are neatly separate. In the Preface to *Annus Mirabilis* Dryden betrayed, in the very act of talking about the imagination making images, what he did not understand about imaging. Having described the imagination as a nimble spaniel hunting its quarry in the field of memory, he added "or, without metaphor, . . . [the imagination] searches over all the memory for the species or ideas of those things which it designs to represent" (Watson, I, *98*). It did not occur to him that there is anything metaphorical about "searches over." He did not see how constitutive metaphor is in language's history, or how inevitably we represent the nonspatial in spatial terms.

The unconsciousness is not a temporary lapse; it accords with his general notion of language, in which figurative and literal are felt as sharply distinct. To put it in (ugly but useful) modern jargon, Dryden felt that all vehicles are translatable to tenor, and that no tenor relies for its real existence on vehicle. Such a view leads him to put things too lucidly (to make them more lucid than reality) in talking of imagery, of metaphors, of style, of the steps of the making, and more generally of design.[24] But if such views limit, they also have virtues. Perspicuity can be luminous, and his sense of the practice of poetry, the rich singularity of its truly proper motions, softens and infiltrates what is stiff in his theory. As he said in "A Discourse concerning Satire," there is a "mystery of that noble trade, which yet no master can teach to his apprentice; he may give the rules, but

9

the scholar is never the nearer in his practice" (Watson, II, *137*).

In the very phrase "disposing of actions and passions" there is a sense which the poet had, even when the theorist did not, that much of the real unity of a poem comes within the working between action and passion, character and language, figure and thought. The design of poetry is not abstract structure *plus* style and figures, though it is fair to add that more modern views of structure which underplay extrinsic shaping are apt to justify chaos.[25] Dryden's ability to "dispose" is better than such passages of his criticism would suggest. The shaping hand is often wiser than the asking mind.

His view of the place of morality in design may sometimes sound rigid, as in a passage in "A Parallel Betwixt Painting and Poetry": "For the moral (as Bossu observes) is the first business of the poet, as being the groundwork of his instruction. This being formed, he contrives such a design, or fable, as may be most suitable to the moral. After this he begins to think of the persons whom he is to employ in carrying on his design; and gives them the manners which are most proper to their several characters. The thoughts and words are the last parts, which give beauty and coloring to the piece" (Watson, II, *186*).

This appears as stodgily didactic and overschematic as one may wish, but another comment on Bossu in the Preface to *Troilus and Cressida* opens the meaning: " 'Tis the moral that directs the whole action of the play to one centre; and that action or fable is the example built upon the moral, which confirms the truth of it to our experience" (Watson, I, *248*).

10

Dryden means in the passage such plain, overt, and abstract morals as Homer's "that union preserves a commonwealth, and discord destroys it" and Sophocles' "that no man is to be accounted happy before his death," and he goes on to drub home the chronological sense involved: "then, and not before, the persons are to be introduced." Yet in the idea, and Dryden's more supple handling of it in his practice and the hints and shadings of his best theory, there is something else. To versify a moral abstraction is one thing, and we tend to flinch away from or laugh at a theory that insists on it. But to arrive at a moral unity of tone, or to have a genuinely unifying purpose, is another thing. If we think of the quality of *pietas* in Virgil and Aeneas, or the dark and strange serenity of spirit in Sophocles and Oedipus of *Oedipus at Colonus*, we realize that the notion is far from trivial. Such qualities are moral and theological and do deeply affect the unity of a work. The great and much celebrated images in Shakespeare's structures are active, sequential, moral, and ontological. In some sense, to say that the unity of a work resides in its tone is virtually tautologous, since "tone" can and does mean the spirit of the work, as we respond to it: our whole and essential response to the felt and total and pervasive quality of a work. If that lacks, the work is disunified, almost by definition. Tone is, to brazen out the metaphor, the outward and invisible sign of an inward and structural strength, a truth that Aristotle himself slighted, and that Bossu and Dryden, however clumsily, touched on. And, while such tone is not exhausted by the moral abstractions consonant with it, such abstractions have importance as measures of and gestures at such

11

moral unity. A moral vision is not a gadget, or a simple inference, but it can be discussed, and in some part paraphrased. Theme matters. Why? Because, as one of the greatest of poets and critics has told us, a poet is a man speaking to men.

Further, certain kinds of poems, a poem such as *Absalom and Achitophel* or a satire as described by Dryden,[26] do have unifying purposes that can be simply stated: a cause is defended or a vice attacked. In such poems the confirming of the truth of the "one centre" is crucial to form. At his best, Dryden is not clumsy about such things. "Poesy must resemble natural truth, but it must *be* ethical." [27] The ways in which poems become and are ethical truth are more varied and more unifying than the theory of the rhetoricians and Bossu. Dryden accepted those theories and was limited by them, but reaches beyond the limits in some of his criticism, often in critical metaphors that say more than his theory of metaphor would allow. One of the best of such metaphors is in *An Essay of Dramatic Poesy*. Neander is speaking of plot and subplot, but the image catches Dryden's fuller sense of what mystery and harmony a "great design" may have, a design proper to the rich mystery and intelligibility of the nature poetry seeks.

> [English plays] have under-plots . . . which are carried on with the motion of the main plot; just as they say the orb of the fixed stars, and those of the planets, though they have motions of their own, are whirled about by the motion of the *primum mobile*, in which they are contained. That similitude expresses much of the English stage; for if contrary motions may be found in nature to agree; if a planet can go east and

west at the same time, one way by virtue of his own
motion, the other by the force of the First Mover, . . .
the under-plot . . . may naturally be conducted along
with [the main design].[28]

The motions of design are more than an abstraction can
handle; and the parts and elements of a poem do not sit
side by untouching side, a truth Dryden at theory too
often forgets, but remembers or learns in such passages
as the one above and as another in the same essay (also
borrowing, as Dryden was fond of doing, an analogy
from science): "What the philosophers say of motion,
that, when it is once begun it continues of itself, and will
do so to eternity without some stop put to it, is clearly
true [of plays], . . . the soul, being already moved with
the characters and fortunes of those imaginary persons,
continues going of its own accord" (Watson, I, *52*).
What moves the souls of the audience is an essential part
of the real unity of the poem, and that "what" does not
reduce to abstracted action or character. It is a full
response to what is fully present in the style and meanings of the play. A similar recognition appears in the
Preface to *Troilus and Cressida,* in which he says that
the poet should have a "knowledge of the passions, what
they are in their own nature, and by what springs they
are to be moved," and that he should "observe the crisis
and turns of them, in their cooling and decay" (Watson,
I, *254*). The crisis and turns are much of the "what" to
which the soul of the listener responds.

Another metaphor, a traditional one given a special
turn, shows that the genuine unity of a poem is involved
in the conventions and singularities of the making.
"Judgment is indeed the master-workman in a play; but

he requires many subordinate hands, many tools to his assistance. And verse I affirm to be one of these: 'tis a rule and line by which he keeps his building compact and even, which otherwise lawless imagination would raise either irregularly or loosely." [29] Judgment checking the irregularities of fancy, while it holds a (partly tautologous) truth, is not the most exciting of critical ideas. But the metaphor shows a recognition of a truth which this study depends on and concerns: that verse is structure, and that it helps make structure. This is one of the ideas deepest in Dryden's feeling for poetry, though it seldom appears in open theory. His sense of form is deeply integral with his sense of versification, which is his greatest poetic power and leads to some of his finest critical statements (all in all, finer than his statements about design). Dryden was proud of his versification, as he might be.

He wrote in the Postscript to the Reader of his translation of the *Aeneid:* "Somewhat (give me leave to say) I have added to both of them [the language and poetry of England] in the choice of words, and harmony of numbers, which were wanting, especially the last, in all our poets, even in those who, being endued with genius, yet have not cultivated their mother-tongue with sufficient care; or, relying on the beauty of their thoughts, have judged the ornament of words, and sweetness of sound, unnecessary" (Watson, II, *258–59*).

The phrasing may make the claim appear more modest than it is. The words "even in those" exclude no great poet, not Chaucer nor Spenser nor Milton nor Shakespeare. Yet he made the claim not in boldness, but in candor. He had devoted a lifetime of hard labor to improving the diction and versification of his language, and he was willing to stand by the result, in his theory and his practice.

Dryden's theory of versification involves two ideals: harmony and propriety. Versification should be harmonious, musical, and sweet.[30] Yet it should also be proper to subject.[31] Harmony and propriety are in some respects natural enemies,[32] the ideal of harmony tending to set versification free from all but its own inner laws, the ideal of propriety demanding that versification be fitted to meaning. Yet both ideals are in accord with Dryden's general theory of poetry, that poetry be a just and lively image of nature. Rules of prosody are possible because natural and permanent accords exist between human nature and the laws of harmony. And propriety of versification to subject is essential if poetry is to imitate nature justly. The contrasting claims of harmony and propriety are real, and overlapping; Dryden mediates them. If he does not finally resolve the claims of the intrinsic and extrinsic values of versification, no later critic has either.[33] Dryden, more than any other critic in English, avoids the sharp edges of the dilemma, by critical tact and a cultivated awareness of the actual workings of poetry.

The ideal of harmony as a separate and intrinsic good made possible the *Prosodia* (now lost) of Dryden,[34] and the rules scattered through his criticism which R. D. Jameson draws together.[35] Dryden's emphasis is on smoothness, variety, and vigor, on restricted enjambment, on "cadency" (the total rhythmic value of lines), on the avoidance of synaloepha (unelided vowels side by side in separate syllables), and on the avoidance of accidental cacophony. He gives careful rules for control of feet, accents, and syllables. The purpose of such rules is

15

to help the poet achieve harmony, to help him order sound into patterns pleasing in themselves.

The ideal of propriety underlies the need to choose numbers appropriate to the various genres, to echo sense in sound, to govern rhyme by sense. He mediates the claims of harmony and propriety in the Preface to *Tyrannic Love:* "By the harmony of words we elevate the mind to a sense of devotion, as our solemn music, which is inarticulate poesy, does in churches" (Watson, I, *139*).

The harmony affects those passions of the audience which have natural affinities with the subject; therefore the effect is proper to the subject. That theory is a sound one and one which shows that Dryden's belief in imitative harmony involved more than a penchant for playing with onomatopoeic sounds.[36] In his notion of imitative harmony, the ideas of harmony and propriety meet.

In the Preface to *Sylvae,* Dryden censures the critics and imitators who idolize some popular poet and cannot tell when the poet's "thoughts are improper to his subject, or his expressions unworthy of his thoughts, or [when] the turn of both is unharmonious" (Watson, II, *20*). Here again, propriety and harmony are interwoven; metrics are closely allied to thought and expression, especially by the metaphor "turn."

His criticism displays many such alliances. In the Preface to *Annus Mirabilis*, he says that versification should be "apt, significant, and sounding" (Watson, I, *98*). In *An Essay of Dramatic Poesy*, all speakers agree that rhyme "should never mislead the sense, but itself be led and governed by it" (Watson, I, *25*). In the Preface to *Sylvae,* he says that "the ear must preside, and direct the judgment to the choice of numbers."[37] Hardly a passage on versification in Dryden's work fails to discover a balance that allies but does not confuse ear and judgment, sense and sound, a balance that is seldom betrayed either to formula or caprice.

Yet Dryden was also quite conscious of how inadequate the best theory was to formulate his real understanding of the subject. In a passage from the Preface to *Sylvae* (part of which I have just quoted), his awareness of that inadequacy is made plain: "[The] ear must preside, and direct the judgment to the choice of numbers: without the nicety of this, the harmony of Pindaric verse can never be complete; the cadency of one line must be a rule to that of the next; and the sound of the former must slide gently into that which follows, without leaping from one extreme into another. It must be done like the shadowings of a picture, which fall by degrees into a darker colour. I shall be glad, if I have so explained myself as to be understood; but if I have not, *quod nequeo dicere, et sentio tantum,* must be my excuse" (Watson, II, *32–33*).[38]

The ear that presides over judgment rules a nicety of balance. Judgment must yield to experience, to the ear that realizes more than theory can trace, yet the judgment does not thereby submit to irrationality or caprice. Dryden does not theorize; he judges, and his judgment leans on graceful metaphor as much as on abstraction. The shadows slide gently on each other.

Another example is a couplet in the beautiful poem *To the Memory of Mr. Oldham,* a poem in which the relative claims of nature (native talent) and art (the learned labor of the craftsman) are a major theme. Nature is felt to be peculiarly the power of the young, art of the mature. A strong feeling runs through the poem that

17

youth's fire is nobler, and better for satire, than the more settled judgment of maturity. Yet the poem contradicts that feeling. Harshness, if noble, is still harsh; maturity has its rights; the numbers of the native tongue are very important. The opposition of the claims is hardly felt as self-inconsistency, even when stated as oxymoron, as in "noble Error." The balance is delicately kept: "Wit will shine / Through the harsh cadence of a rugged line" (vv. 15–16).

Dryden means primarily that wit (here both general intellectual power and the salted lash of satiric ingenuity) will manifest itself in spite of rough versification: it will shine through it as sun shines through fog; but there is a hint that wit is enforced in satire by a proper harshness, that "through" means "by the agency of." The hint is itself enforced by the imitative ruggedness of "harsh cadence" and "rugged line." [39] Youthful fire, for all its improprieties, is more to be admired than the polish that comes with age; yet, in a way, force is *not* improper: it is, in its very violence, proper to the moods of satire. One hardly feels the tension between the contrary implications, so gracefully are they turned to praise; but the tension is there. Dryden here as elsewhere adjusts the contrary claims of propriety and harmony as well as those of nature and art.

Dryden is never more conscious of the true work of metrics than when he thinks of the versification of Virgil.[40] In the Preface to *Annus Mirabilis,* he says most powerfully, what he is virtually to repeat in the Preface to *Sylvae* (Watson, II, *21*) and the Dedication of the *Aeneid* (Watson, II, *235*): "the very sound of his words have often somewhat that is connatural to the subject" (Watson, I, *100*). *Connatural* is a strong word. It not only intensifies *natural,* but it also means "congenital" and "innate," strongly suggesting the most profound connections of birth, descent, and essence. The word *somewhat* is a sign of mystery, a mystery for which Dryden felt a deep and continued respect and which he sought to explore with candor and modesty. More important, he attempted throughout his long devoted life to realize the "connatural" in his poetry. It was not only a reasonable but a luminous search.

In important ways the key to Dryden's poetry is versification. Modern readers are used to shocks of diction, involutions or fragmentations of syntax, intricacies of metaphor. In Dryden they will find little of such technique; his diction is clear and pure, his syntax normally straightforward, his imagery precise, often warm and glowing but not often interpenetrative with idea. When it penetrates, it enters as sun enters water. But that does not mean that Dryden shapes his poetic thought less precisely or less intricately than other poets. It means that he makes or strengthens many of his finer adjustments of thought and feeling with his versification. It takes some listening to learn to follow his metrical ways. They are ways to which few modern ears are accustomed. But the rewards are well worth the listening; to hear him out is to discover an excellent poetic world.

2

The Very Sound: A Study of Imitative Harmony

THE DOCTRINE AND PRACTICE of imitative harmony (of the neoclassical writers in general and Dryden in particular) have been much disprized,[1] even by critics who in general admire Dryden's versification. Mark Van Doren, who elsewhere in his book praises Dryden for his "great ear,"[2] is extremely harsh: "At its highest, imitative harmony cannot be said to have attained the dignity of an art. It was always a cheap and easy artifice not to be associated with that mysterious power, possessed in abundance by Virgil, Shakespeare, Milton, and Wordsworth, which works its mighty will among the emotions through sound *and* sense."[3]

Mere direct imitations of sound and motion, which are what Van Doren understands Dryden to mean by imitative harmony, are in themselves no great matter. But to see imitative harmony only there is seriously limiting. Dryden set no such limits. He had a firm understanding of what sound may and may not do, an understanding rooted in the doctrine of propriety to nature. Human nature for Dryden is not casual, nor its passions trivial. In his doctrine, art's very existence depends on natural (aesthetically real and metaphysically founded) accords between art, subject, and audience. Dryden's theory explores those accords. So does his practice, in richly singular ways that illuminate and specify his theory. To understand that practice, we need to see ways in which sound and sense work together.

A passage in Samuel Johnson attacking imitative harmony suggests one of the most important: "The fancied resemblances, I fear, arise sometimes merely from the ambiguity of words; there is supposed to be some relation between a *soft* line and a *soft* couch, or between *hard* syllables and *hard* fortune." [4]

That statement is manifestly inconsistent with what Johnson says elsewhere, as when he censures Dryden for wishing that Butler had written in heroic couplets: "If he [Dryden] intended that when the numbers were heroick the diction should still remain vulgar, he planned a very heterogeneous and unnatural composition. If he preferred a general stateliness both of sound and words, he can be only understood to wish Butler had undertaken a different work." [5]

"Heroic" and "stately" are not mere ambiguities, meaning one thing for numbers and another for actions. As Johnson knew, the human mind detects some like quality in heroic numbers and heroic action. *Paradise Lost* could not have been written in limericks. And if heroic, why not soft? After all, lines are said to be "soft"

21

by a metaphor to physical softness, a metaphor applied because people feel a like quality in soft lines and soft couches. And if versification can imitate through a metaphor to softness, why not through a metaphor to sound or motion? And what can not be compared to sound and motion, with their coordinates of time and place? As soon as one admits that versification and subject can share *any* like qualities, the possibilities for liaisons between sense and sound become many.

Simple onomatopoeia, words which sound what they name, is admitted by even those critics most suspicious of imitative harmony. Such onomatopoeia, directly applied, may be obtrusive, and is in its nature uncommon: poems only seldom speak of creatures that thump or hiss or buzz or hum. There are, however, subtler varieties, for instance the word "sparkle," which somehow sounds the appearance of what it names. And something near to simple onomatopoeia, applied metaphorically or obliquely to meaning, may be of the substance of good poetry.

Van Doren admires Dryden's description of the enthusiasts in *Absalom and Achitophel* ("A numerous Host of dreaming Saints succeed; / Of the true old Enthusiastick breed" [vv. 529–30]). Of it he writes that "the vowels and the consonants, whether or not they were thoughtfully chosen, are steeped in disdain." [6] So they are; in large part because the sounds, especially the *s*'s, *t*'s, *d*'s and the explosive *b* of "breed," are very responsive to the accents of disdain. Disdain is one, though it is but one, of the potentialities of those sounds. We *hiss* and *sputter* when angry and contemptuous. The sounds do not directly imitate the subject, the enthusiasts, but they help to create the proper attitude of contempt toward the subject. They are proper to the subject.

Sound imitates physical force so naturally that it is hard to talk of light and heavy stress without using a metaphor of force, as the words *light* and *heavy* themselves attest. More important, meter and meaning affect each other reciprocally. Both of these truths are exemplified in a verse from Dryden's translation, in *The Third Miscellany,* of the Fable of Acis, Polyphemus, and Galatea from Ovid's *Metamorphoses:* "This airy walk, the Giant Lover chose" (v. 51). Air is light; a giant is heavy. The word *airy* is a distinctly light two syllables, the word *giant* heavier and lengthened and deepened by context. The comedy of the passage from which this verse is taken comes largely from the incongruity of the heavy Polyphemus attempting the light ways of love.

Similar effects occur in more serious places, as in Dryden's fine translation of Horace's Ode 29 of the Third Book.

> I can enjoy her [Fortune] while she's kind;
> But when she dances in the wind,
> And shakes her wings, and will not stay,
> I puff the Prostitute away.
>
> (vv. 81–84)

The passage is easy and delicate in rhythm. *Puff,* formally an onomatopoeic word, is very light and suggests the gaiety with which virtue overcomes fortune. The lightness by its lightness shows moral strength.

The context of sound and meaning can radically change the force of a word, for example the word *storm(s)* in the last stanza of the same translation.

> What is't to me,
> Who never sail in her [Fortune's] unfaithful Sea,
> If Storms arise, and Clouds grow black;
> If the Mast split and threaten wreck
>
> (vv. 88–91)

> In my small Pinnace I can sail,
> Contemning all the blustring roar;
> And running with a merry gale,
> With friendly Stars my safety seek
> Within some little winding Creek;
> And see the storm a shore.
>
> (vv. 99–104)

In verses 90–91, the *storms* (like the *clouds*) is fiercely said, the pronunciation drawn out, the sharp *black-wreck* rhyme and the mouthed struggle of the harsh and hard-to-say *mast split* intensifying the effect. In verses 99–104 the context, including the light words *little* and *see*, diminishes force and *storm* becomes a much softer word, and thing, than it was in the previous passage. It has been quietened by perspective, by the context of sound, and by rational calm.

The words *mast split* illustrate that sound in relation to meaning is a phenomenon of the mouth as well as of the ear. An amusing and unmistakable example of this relationship occurs in a passage in *The Medal*, where the mouth is part of the subject (emphasis mine):

> The Man who laugh'd but once, to see an Ass
> *Mumbling* to make the *cross-grain'd Thistles* pass;
> Might laugh again, to see a Jury chaw
> The *prickles of unpalatable* Law.
>
> (vv. 145–48)

24

Back diphthongs have a resonance which in proper context can become poetically meaningful. Dryden is fond of *ound* rhymes and uses them well, nowhere more powerfully than in the close of his great elegy *To the Memory of Mr. Oldham:*

> Thy Brows with Ivy, and with Laurels bound;
> But Fate and gloomy Night encompass thee around.
>
> (vv. 24–25)

The rhyme is strengthened by *m-n* linkages, and echoes darkly. To encompass is to encompass around, yet the tautology is not wasted. The gloom of death is not merely an encircling: it moves out of itself in the strangeness of its realm.

Meter helps to establish general conventions of feeling and to adapt those conventions to fine nuances of meaning. Most critics will grant that certain measures are more appropriate to certain kinds of poetry than are others: we may think of blank verse, heroic couplets, ballad stanzas, typical song measures, galloping or lilting anapestic measures, limericks, the complex and soaring patterns of the great odes. Furthermore, meter can make fine adjustments of feeling, a function which mock-epic, with its numerous ways of playing off tone against subject, neatly illustrates. Meter is capable of these adjustments, because sound patterns can affect emotion (some music is gay, some solemn) and because poems convey emotions about subjects.

The most important way in which meter affects meaning is by emphasis, stressing certain words and relating certain stresses and words to each other. The power of meter to emphasize and relate words can be illustrated

25

almost anywhere in poetry. I take one example from *The Second Part of Absalom and Achitophel,* and one from William Browne.

When Dryden writes of Og (emphasis his),

> The Midwife laid her hand on his Thick Skull,
> With this Prophetick blessing—*Be thou Dull;*
> (vv. 476–77)

we are not apt to forget the dullness which the rhyme and the concentration of accent help to force on our attention. The italics speak the tune.

Or, in Browne's famous Epitaph on the Countess of Pembroke, the line "Fair and learn'd and good as she," by meter, as by syntax and by meaning, relates the qualities of beauty and wisdom and goodness to the lady. The four stressed words are "Fair-learn'd-good-she."

Relations between elements of versification can suggest similar relations between elements of subject. In Campion's translation "My sweetest Lesbia, let us live and love," the alliteration has its melodic work. The words "live" and "love" do more. They are very alike, both in sound and in the prominence the meter gives them. The meter helps to identify them with each other. That identity of living and loving is the substance of the poem. The metrical relations imitate and further the relations of meaning.

It is well known that the heroic couplet is highly appropriate to antithesis and balance, which may stress comparison or contrast of meaning. Critics seldom think of that relation as imitative harmony, but it is. The relation also shows another important fact: parallelism or antithesis each can show comparison or contrast or other relations. They force certain words into a clear metrical and syntactical relation to each other: if their meanings clash, the clash is stressed; if their meanings are alike, the likeness is stressed. The meter says, in effect, "Attend to these words: they are closely related." The mind then perceives what the relation is.

Four verses from *Absalom and Achitophel* exemplify at least three different functionings of metrical parallelism.

> What cannot Praise effect in Mighty Minds,
> When Flattery Sooths, and when Ambition Blinds!
> Desire of Power, on earth a Vitious Weed,
> Yet, sprung from High, is of Caelestial Seed:
> (vv. 303–306)

The metrical (and syntactical) parallelism of "Flattery" and "Ambition" stresses their likeness; the metrical (though not syntactical) parallelism of "Vitious Weed" and "Caelestial Seed" stresses their radical unlikeness. The metrical parallelism of "Minds" and "Blinds" shows a strong relation that is neither comparison nor contrast.

Again in *Absalom and Achitophel,* metrical parallelism shows an intended comparison in "No *King* could govern, nor no *God* could please" (v. 48). It shows contrast in verse 44, "Heaven punishes the *bad,* and proves the *best.*"

In an octosyllabic couplet of Donne's *Valediction Forbidding Mourning,* metrical parallelism stresses both comparison and contrast (since things unlike are being paradoxically identified):

> Thy firmness makes my circle just,
> And makes me *end,* where I *begun.*

27

The reverse occurs in *The Hind and the Panther*, part I. Two occurences of the same idea are contrasted: The Hind had been *"doom'd* [by men] to death, though *fated* [by God] not to dy" (v. 8).[7] The metrical stress, the grammatical parallelism, the *t-d* linkage (*d*oom'*d* *t*o *d*eath fa*ted* no*t* *t*o *d*y), and the paradox inherent in "fated not to dy"—all enforce the contrast of time and eternity.

In summary, the relations between metrics and meaning are many. Sound and sense may share analogous qualities (softness and stateliness, for example). Sound can plainly suggest sound, speed, motion, weight, and anything that can be understood in a metaphor of sound, speed, motion, or weight. Harmony of sound can affect our passions and feelings, both in helping to establish a general tone and by adjusting feeling closely to particular ideas. Certain sounds are appropriate to expressing certain attitudes. Meter is very important in stressing meaning, and relations of sound or meter can imitate or suggest analogous relations.

One must insist, again, that sound has very few of these effects independent of meaning; it has them in complex conjunction with meaning; sound can affect meaning, as meaning can affect sound. One more illustration of the reciprocity of that relation may be useful. The sound *ickle* has considerable comic potential. Whether that potential is realized will depend on context: the comic potential is realized in the slang "pickle face." It is realized in these lines from a song by Dryden from *Amphitryon:* "She's fickle and false, and there we agree; / For I am as false, and as fickle as she." It is, most definitely, *not* realized in one of Shakespeare's greatest lines: "Within his bending sickle's compass come." Yet Shakespeare himself probably could not have used *ickle* as a rhyme without releasing the lurking comedy. The context and abstract meaning help determine how much of the metrical meaning will be realized. One may reverse that statement. Sound affects sense; sense affects sound. Dryden mastered both.

3

A Myrtle Shade:
The Songs of Dryden

DRYDEN'S SONGS ARE in an astonishing variety of different measures.[1] He uses as a basis for songs[2] anapests, iambs, trochees, dactyls, mixtures of two or more of these feet, an ambiguous seven-syllable measure (a famous Elizabethan example is Browne's "Underneath this sable hearse") which can be scanned as iambic with the first foot truncated or as trochaic with the final foot truncated. He also uses dipodic rhythm, and in some of his best songs combines two metrical systems under tension. He employs many line-feet arrangements, stanzaic patterns, and rhyme schemes. Nor is that variety a mere labor of virtuosity. Dryden tunes almost perfectly each instrument he handles.

Yet, if his control is splendid, his subject often is not. Most of his songs are of love, a diminished love. Where once the physical union was seen by poets as a symbol of the spiritual bond and as the proper completion of a complex ritual, spiritual gestures are, in the Restoration "courtly" view, but a clever means for a seducer to use. Restoration songs typically speak of the physical union or of the means to achieve it.

The real objection to the typical Restoration lyric is less to the sensuality than to the narrowness. No longer a motive for great enterprise, as in the medieval world of Chaucer's *Troilus and Cressida,* nor an analogue, at times noble, at times blasphemous, to the spiritual, as in Donne, nor a means of revelation of the glories and evils of the human spirit, as supremely in Shakespeare's sonnets, Restoration "love" is seldom better than trivial. Even when, as in some of Congreve's work, it is decent, it is hardly profound or transforming. The great exception is Dryden's *All for Love.*

There is no reason to condone what Dryden himself more than once condemned, most famously in the Anne Killigrew Ode, where he speaks of the "lubrique and adul'trate age," and in the Preface to the Fables. His lyrics are often flawed in substance by the view of human personality that Restoration "love" implies. But Dryden's lyrics can be varied and oblique in their relations to Restoration "love"; they attain at times considerable excellence of substance as well as of form. One of his ways of creating the substance is by using supple metrical control.

Many of the songs are borne up by a buoyant wit that, in making comedy out of sensuality, lessens its force as sensuality. Sometimes they reflect the better conventions of a previous time. Song 1 in *An Evening's Love* begins with two lines that might have come from Jonson or Campion:

You charm'd me not with that fair face
   Though it was all divine:
To be anothers is the Grace,
   That makes me wish you mine.

The poem is in one of the most common lyric measures, and the first two lines by their smoothness, connotation, slow sweetness of movement, and diction create a rich image of praise for a lady. One expects higher praise to follow (that it was her spiritual rather than her physical beauty that won him) and gets a shock. One may call this mock-lyric: the style and substance are in deliberate conflict. In this stanza one witnesses the undoing of a great lyric tradition.

Less curious mixtures of sentiment appear in such happy and saucy pieces as Song 4 in *An Evening's Love* ("Celimena, of my heart") and Mercury's Song to Phaedra in *Amphitryon* ("Fair *Iris* I love, and hourly I dye"), where the wit is sustained by a bouncy metrical pattern.

The seduction pieces are often well made. Only one is very sensual in feeling and it is one of the best. The Zambra Dance from *The Conquest of Granada*, moves with a sleepy sensuality deeply involved in the changing line lengths, the winding enjambment, in the three rhyming verses at the end of each stanza that open from a tetrameter couplet to a pentameter verse which, at least in the first two stanzas, is as slow and languorous in effect as almost any hexameter.

Undress'd she came my flames to meet,
While Love strow'd flow'rs beneath her feet;
Flow'rs, which so press'd by her, became more sweet.
                       (vv. 5–7)

> Her hands, her lips did love inspire;
> Her every grace my heart did fire:
> But most her eyes which languish'd with desire.
>
> (vv. 12–14)

The repetition, the climactic concentration on one "charm" after another, the virtually isochronic feet of the first verse, the heavy accents slowed by such heavy unaccented syllables as "strow'd," the repetition of the long "flow'rs," the pause on either side of "which so press'd by her," the imitatively long and slow word "languish'd"—all these do not make, just in themselves, the melody of the passion, but they are deeply involved in it at each slow stage of the dance.

Many of the pieces about seduction or the act of love are well tuned with a flowing and good-humored prettiness that almost belies the subject. Notable among these are Song 3 from *An Evening's Love* ("Calm was the Even, and cleer was the skie") and the anapestic "A New Song" ("Sylvia the fair, in the bloom of Fifteen"). Even Song 2 from *Marriage a la Mode* ("Whil'st *Alexis* lay prest"), with its turbulent and brilliant motion (it is about the timing of coition), comes nearer in effect to gay and pretty comedy than to the salacious.[3] Such poems are not directly sensual; they encourage sensuality by finding it an amusing pastime in an artificial world.

That world has its artifice of nature, a nature which has been smoothened and generalized for the ladies by meter and by rhetoric. One should not, Dryden once smilingly affirmed, perplex ladies with complex truths; one should "entertain them with the softnesses of love."[4] The formula for the entertainment is given in Damilcar's

song "You pleasing dreams of Love and sweet delight" in
Tyrannic Love; it is in the play, as elsewhere, a formula
for seduction:

> Let purling streams be in her fancy seen;
> And flowry Meads, and Vales of chearful green.
>
> (vv. 9–10)

The trochaic and unsurprising epithets, typical of one
(though it is only one) kind of neoclassical diction for
describing nature, are there because they are conventional and because trochaic words flow nicely in iambic
patterns. A dance is a convention, this convention the
dance of a game. Dryden knows exactly what he is
doing: the physical nature so smoothened is not meant
as a true image of the actual phenomena of the world.
The language is highly selective, proper to certain light
feelings. It is often dull, often pleasant. At its best, it
becomes lovely, as in a songlike passage in Prologue to
The Dutchess:

> For Her the weeping Heav'ns become serene,
> For Her the Ground is clad in cheerfull green:
> For Her the Nightingales are taught to sing,
> And Nature has for her delay'd the Spring.
>
> (vv. 26–29)

Saintsbury has remarked the lively handling of the pronoun.[5] One may add that its repetition, thrice in the same
place, once in a central place, plays against the movement, center to end to center, of the repeated metrical
pattern in "weeping Heav'ns," "cheerfull green," and
"Nightingales." Art shows art, and the deliberately unreal nature goes beyond prettiness (as it frequently does
when Dryden writes of beauty and social hierarchy); it

touches an original and paradisaic freshness. The versification, like the moment of real myth (it is Nature who delays the spring, Nature who controls nature) gives a sweetness of life to the conventional language.

The formula of "Nature methodized" is too pat to show what Dryden is doing with such language. He is not merely selecting from nature to make an elegant object of art; rather, the language reflects a reality of nature as his poetics conceived it: beauty, including the beauty of ladies, is real. To be beautiful, to be real, is to be of nature in a most fundamental sense. Nature includes natural law, the natural law which artistic truth implies and which Dryden always, even when smiling, affirms.

To flirt consciously with what one considers immoral is also, in its way, to affirm natural law, and strange blends occur. Delicacy of tone may hide Restoration indelicacies, as in a song in *Troilus and Cressida* ("Can life be a blessing"), a song from *King Arthur* ("How happy the Lover"), and a song from *Tyrannic Love* ("Ah how sweet it is to love"). The last of these shows how Dryden can make various music by exploiting the ambiguities of a metrical system. I quote the first and third stanzas.

> Ah how sweet it is to love,
> Ah how gay is young desire!
> And what pleasing pains we prove
> When we first approach Loves fire!
>   Pains of Love be sweeter far
>   Than all other pleasures are.
>   (vv. 1–6)

> Love and Time with reverence use,
> Treat 'em like a parting friend:

> Nor the golden gifts refuse
> Which in youth sincere they send:
>   For each year their price is more,
>   And they less simple than before.
>   (vv. 13–18)

In the first stanza, each of the first four lines seems to begin with an anapestic motion that slows to the iambs. If the first stanza stood alone, we might well scan each of them a i i: [6]

| Ah how sweet | it is | to love |

It is a nice pattern: more lilting than straight iambs, less jingly and hence richer than an unchecked anapestic flow. "Pains of Love" reads as a variation on the pattern, possibly a cretic substitution. The emphasis on "Pains" is strong and harmonically pleasant, proper to a pain that is really a pleasure. The "than" of the last line of the stanza is also ambiguous in accent, though less so than "Pains." We may expect that something is amiss here, because the cretic (stressed, unstressed, stressed) is virtually nonexistent as an English foot. The later stanzas show what is amiss.

The basic line shape, we discover, is not an anapest followed by two iambs, but truncated tetrameter, which can be read as iambic or trochaic. In the first four lines of the third stanza, the relatively strong stress on the first syllable makes the stanza move more slowly than did the first stanza. As befits the varying speeds, the third stanza is more meditative, the first stanza more gay.

Having found the real base of the poem, we learn that the first stanza fits it. The first syllable of each of the first four lines is light enough to serve as the unaccented syllable of an anapest; but, since it is stronger than the second syllable, it can also serve as a truncated foot and the lines can then be scanned to fit the base:

| Ah | how sweet | it is | to love | x i i i
| Ah how | sweet it | is to | love | t t t x

The metrical resolution does not change the contrast of effect; the first stanza is flowing and sweet; the third stanza is slower and more mellow,[7] in part because the stanzas have been turned in different metrical directions within the framework of a single comprehensible system.

Some of Dryden's songs, including the best ones, have a primary metrical base that sustains some strong competition from another base. Especially susceptible to such flexibility is the eleven-syllable line.[8] Song 2 from *An Evening's Love* (which alternates eleven-syllable and ten-syllable lines) is in subject, and in some part in treatment, gay and lightly sensual; it is in other ways a puzzling poem.

I

After the pangs of a desperate Lover,
When day and night I have sigh'd all in vain,
Ah what a pleasure it is to discover
In her eyes pity, who causes my pain!

II

When with unkindness our love at a stand is,
And both have punish'd our selves with the pain,
Ah what a pleasure the touch of her hand is,
Ah what a pleasure to press it again!

III

When the denyal comes fainter and fainter,
And her eyes give what her tongue does deny,
Ah what a trembling I feel when I venture,
Ah what a trembling does usher my joy!

IV

When, with a Sigh, she accords me the blessing,
And her eyes twinkle 'twixt pleasure and pain;
Ah what a joy 'tis, beyond all expressing,
Ah what a joy to hear, shall we again!

The poem should be mildly salacious and amusing like the song "Whil'st *Alexis* lay prest," but it touches unexpected feelings. The metrical base can be described most simply as falling, but changes occur.

The first line typifies the odd lines, dactylic tetrameter with a trochee in the fourth place: [9]

| After the | pangs of a | desperate | Lover | d d d t

No even line is absolutely unambiguous in movement. Line 8, if "Ah" receives considerable more stress than "what," shows the pattern, dactylic tetrameter with fourth foot truncated:

| Ah what a | pleasure to | press it a | gain! | d d d x

If in a ten-syllable line, the first syllable is weaker, the tendency is to a straight rising line, i i a a, as in one natural and possible, though not exclusive, reading of line 2:

| When day | and night | I have sigh'd | all in vain |

The possibility of variant and crossing rhythm is large, moving toward iambic pentameter, as in the last line: [10]

| Ah what | a joy | to hear, || shall we | again! |
t i i | t i

In the first two stanzas, the lilt of the trisyllabic feet prevails and keeps the tone light and gay. In the last two stanzas the feeling becomes more mixed. In the first line of stanza three "comes" threatens or overthrows the normal accent on the *y* of "denyal," makes "comes fainter" of considerable importance, and emphasizes by contrast the imitatively fading rhythm of "fainter and fainter."

| When the de | nyal comes | fainter and | fainter |
d d d t
| When the | deny | al comes | fainter | and faint | er
t i i t i <

In the second verses of the third and fourth stanzas, the pull is strong both ways, the first two feet tending to a pyrrhic-spondaic combination, or to strong and slow iambs.

| And her eyes | give what her | tongue does de | ny |
d d d x
| And her | eyes give | what her tongue | does deny |
p s a a
| And her | eyes give | what her tongue | does deny |
I I a a
| And her eyes | twinkle 'twixt | pleasure and | pain |
d d d x

| And her | eyes twink | le 'twixt plea | sure and pain |
p s a a

| And her | eyes twink | le 'twixt plea | sure and pain |
I I a a

In the last line of the poem, "hear, shall" is strong enough to cross the rhythmic pattern rather bluntly, even clumsily: "Ah what a joy to hear, shall we again!" All in all, the last two stanzas realize, in feeling as in meter, a perturbation that is not merely sexual and that has moments of power. Here, Dryden's meters may be merely confused. The poem is, at best, enigmatic. Yet, whether accident or not, the serious and involved feeling in the third and fourth stanzas is a real potentiality of the crossing of metrical patterns. Elsewhere, Dryden uses similar techniques with mastery.

In two of his finest songs, he plays a trisyllabic base against a disyllabic one in an eleven-syllable line. Those songs are "I feed a flame within, which so torments me" from *Secret Love*, and "No no, poor suff'ring Heart no Change endeavour" from *Cleomenes*.

"I feed a flame within" is iambic, in every line. Yet a dactylic-trochaic pattern is often superimposed and crosses the iambic movement with felicity.

> I feed a flame within which so torments me
> That it both pains my heart, and yet contents me:
> 'Tis such a pleasing smart, and I so love it,
> That I had rather die, then once remove it.
>
> Yet he for whom I grieve shall never know it,
> My tongue does not betray, nor my eyes show it:
> Not a sigh nor a tear my pain discloses,
> But they fall silently like dew on Roses.

Thus to prevent my love from being cruel,
My heart's the sacrifice as 'tis the fuel:
And while I suffer this to give him quiet,
My faith rewards my love, though he deny it.

On his eyes will I gaze, and there delight me;
While I conceal my love, no frown can fright me:
To be more happy I dare not aspire;
Nor can I fall more low, mounting no higher.

The basic pattern is simple: iambic pentameter couplets with feminine endings and with a caesura [11] regularly after the sixth syllable. However, when the first foot is reversed, the line scans most naturally as trochaic pentameter with a dactylic substitution: d t t t t. If the first foot is ambiguous in accent, the rising and falling rhythms are both strongly felt. If the first foot after the caesura is ambiguous (as it often is in this poem), one can scan the five syllables after the caesura as a dactyl and a trochee or as two iambs with feminine ending. The falling rhythm approaches as a limit dactylic tetrameter with a trochee in the last place (d d d t). In short, falling and rising rhythms are poised against each other in the line and the balance may at any moment incline to one or to the other. The possibilities for adjustment between the contrary motions are impressive, and Dryden handles them with exacting control.

The lines of the first stanza fit the iambic norm, but, in the first three lines, there is sufficient accent on the first and seventh syllables for the dactylic rhythm to be felt as a fairly strong counterrhythm.

| I feed | a flame | within || which so | torments | me
i i i | I i <

41

| That it | both pains | my heart, || and yet | contents |
me: i i i | I i <

| 'Tis such | a pleas | ing smart, || and I | so love | it,
                                        i i i | I I <

| That I | had rath | er die, || then once | remove | it.
                                        i i i | i i <

| I feed a | flame within || which so tor | ments me |
                                        d₁ d₂ | d t

| That it both | pains my heart, || and yet con | tents
me: | d₂ d₂ | d t

| 'Tis such a | pleasing smart, || and I so | love it, |
                                        d d₂ | d₁.₂ t

| That I had | rather die, || then once re | move it. |
                                        d d₂ | d t

The first line of the second stanza is iambic, though
the "shall" after the caesura is strong enough to suggest,
if gently, the contrary dactylic motion:

| shall ne | ver know | it   i i <
| shall never | know it | d₁ t

In the second line, the iambic pattern is clear until the
caesura: "nor my" is an ambiguous foot, and "eyes,"
though technically unaccented in either system, is
strong enough to suggest an anapest. The anapestic
movement of "nor my eyes" becomes much plainer in
"Not a sigh nor a tear," which one is tempted to read a a.
Yet the whole weight of the poem works against that
movement. The "not" and the "nor" are ambiguous. One
can read the phrase ("Not a sigh nor a tear") as a
pyrrhic-spondee combination plus an iamb or even as a
trochee, a real spondee,[12] and an iamb, either of which

readings stretch the iambic norm as far as it can go. The rest of the line resolves the intense but quiet struggle into normal iambic movement, preparing for the even more delicately balanced fourth line "But they fall silently like dew on Roses."

| But they | fall si | lently | like dew | on Ros | es.

$$I\ I\ i\ |\ i\ i\ <$$

| But they fall | silently | like dew | on Ros | es.

$$a_{1.2}\ d\ |\ i\ i\ <$$

The first four syllables are all gentle, yet almost equal claimants for accent. The line can be read in straight and unforced iambics, yet the hovering accent allows an anapestic motion to the first three syllables, a motion balanced by the natural dactyl "silently" (which strictly cannot be scanned as a dactyl here, but which nonetheless supplies dactylic motion as a counterrhythm). The "ly," though almost a whisper, is the first syllable in the line that takes the accent quite unambiguously. The rest of the line goes in the most calm iambics. The line is a triumph of quiet: without once raising the metrical voice to a normally strong accent, Dryden suggests by the balanced metrical forces the tremendous muted struggle in the soul of the speaker.

The rest of the poem prepares for the final line, in which there is a statuesque balance of the contrary motions of the poem. In "Nor can I fall more low, mounting no higher," every syllable (except "ing") needed for an iambic reading or for a dactylic reading can receive stress, but the very strong "more low" will not allow either movement to prevail. I would read the line as iambic with two substitutions (t I I | t i <). Other readings are possible; any true reading must suggest the force of the balanced struggle that again echoes and creates the spiritual state of the speaker.

The same metrical norm (iambic eleven-syllable couplets, with caesura regularly after the sixth syllable) serves for a song of Dryden's that has won high praise,[13] "No no, poor suff'ring Heart no Change endeavour" from *Cleomenes*.

> No no, poor suff'ring Heart no Change endeavour,
> Choose to sustain the smart, rather than leave her;
> My ravish'd Eyes behold such Charms about her,
> I can dye with her, but not live without her.
> One tender Sigh of hers to see me Languish,
> Will more than pay the price of my past Anguish:
> Beware O cruel Fair, how you smile on me,
> 'Twas a kind Look of yours that has undone me.
>
> Love has in store for me one happy Minute,
> And She will end my pain who did begin it;
> Then no day void of Bliss, or Pleasure leaving,
> Ages shall slide away without perceiving:
> *Cupid* shall guard the Door the more to please us,
> And keep out Time and Death when they would seize
> us:
> Time and Death shall depart, and say in flying,
> Love has found out a way to Live by Dying.

The first three lines show the iambic and dactylic measures in full competition. The first line scans, with virtually no strain (ignoring secondary accent to show the basic pattern), iambic or dactylic.

> | No   no, | poor   suff | 'ring   Heart || no   Chang | en-
> deav | our,   i i i | i i <

A Myrtle Shade

| No no, poor | suff'ring Heart || no Change en | deav-
our, | d d | d t

The second line is most properly dactylic:

| Choose to sus | tain the smart, || rather than | leave
her | d d₂ | d t

To be read as iambic at all it must be allowed two
trochaic substitutions: t i i | t i <. The third line returns
clearly to the iambic norm, if with a slight hesitation of
accent on "such."

| My ra | vish'd Eyes | behold | such Charms | about |
her   i i i | I i <

The fourth line, separate from context, would appear
mere prose, and even when given metrical shape by the
two norms is as odd in feeling as in metrics and should
probably be counted as a defect. Yet, whether or not
under perfect control, it (like the song "After the pangs
of a desperate Lover") conveys the perturbation of a
lover's mind. I would, with some hesitation, read it as a
badly strained iambic line.

| I can | dye with | her, but | not live | without| her
                                          t I *i* I i <

For once, the falling pattern is felt before, but not after,
the caesura. The dactylic norm is subdued in the remaining lines of the first stanza, whose iambic pattern is
flowing, yet nicely varied:

| One ten | der Sigh | of hers || to see | me Lang | uish,
                                          i i i | i i <

45

| Will   more | than   pay | the   price || of   my | past
Ang | uish: i i i | i I <

| Beware | O cru | el Fair, || how you | smile on | me,
                                        i i i | i I <

| 'Twas a | kind Look | of yours || that has | undone |
me.   t i i | I i <

The second stanza turns away from prettiness. The first
line, like the line that begins the poem, receives strength
from the conjunction of the two metrical norms:

| Love has | in store | for me || one hap | py Min | ute |
                                        i i i | I i <

| Love has in | store for me || one happy | Minute |
                                        d d | d₁ t

The second line is iambic but quickened by a little leap
across the lightly accented "did":

| And She | will end | my pain || who did | begin |it
                                        i i i | *i i* <

The third line begins the rise toward the conclusion.

| Then no | day void | of Bliss, || or Plea | sure leav | ing
                                        i I i | *i i* <

Slowed by six firm accents, and closed by the natural
trochees "pleasure" and "leaving" within the iambic pattern, the line portrays a lingering, almost timeless pleasure. The day of sensation is long, but the years swift,
and the next line catches the quiet speed of their departure.

| Ages | shall slide | away | without | perceiv | ing
                                        t i i | *i i* <

A Myrtle Shade

The light accents are tuned to sliding; no pause breaks the progress. The fifth line of the stanza may fit the basic scansion of the fourth, but the accents are heavy in keeping with a return to the time scale of sensation.

| Cupid | shall guard | the Door || the more | to please | us   t i i | i i <

| Cupid shall | guard the | Door the | more to | please us | d t t t t

In the sixth line, all accented syllables are strong; the unaccented syllables are light in stress but (relatively) long in quantity: the combination is bonded strength.

| And keep | out Time | and Death | when they | would seize | us   i i i | i i <

"Time" and "Death" are boldly repeated in the seventh line, this time in a trochaic pattern, which gives them great metrical emphasis while allowing for the surge of "shall depart" that takes them to their defeat.

| Time and | Death shall | depart, | and say | in fly | ing   t t i | i i <

The rest of the line comes back again, lightly and triumphantly, to the iambic pattern. The last line concludes the poem in a rich iambic flow (the caesura almost vanishing), in which the metrical struggle is suggested by the falling rhythm of "Love has" and "dying." It repeats one of the two possible scansions of the first line of the stanza, rounding out the poem, and repeating in triumph the promise that existed before in hope.

| Love has | found out | a way | to Live | by Dy | ing.   t i i i i <

Yvor Winters writes of this poem that it "is one of the best examples that I know of what can be accomplished by means of meticulous variations from a rigid norm." [14] I have traced those variations in some detail in order to show how the poem realizes its subject. In this poem and in "I feed a flame within," it is very largely the metrical counterpatterning that makes real the torments of love. The "flames" and "pains" and "hearts" and "loves," whose normal range in Restoration verse is from cynical wit to banality, here take on life. Dryden transforms a Restoration convention of love, a convention antisocial and irreligious, into something far better. The love is faithful, not frivolous.

So it is also in "The Lady's Song," a poem which, conventional in almost every detail of language, and extremely regular in its basically anapestic movement, is pervaded by the noble sweetness of spirit of the later Dryden, a sweetness he seldom expressed more eloquently.

THE LADY'S SONG

I

A Quire of bright Beauties in Spring did appear,
To chuse a *May*-Lady to govern the year:
All the Nymphs were in White, and the Shepherds in
    Green,
The Garland was giv'n, and *Phillis* was Queen:
But *Phillis* refus'd it, and sighing did say,
I'll not wear a Garland while *Pan* is away.

II

While *Pan*, and fair *Syrinx*, are fled from our Shore,
The Graces are banish'd, and Love is no more:
The soft God of Pleasure that warm'd our Desires,

Has broken his Bow, and extinguish'd his Fires;
And vows that himself, and his Mother, will mourn,
'Till *Pan* and fair *Syrinx* in Triumph return.

III

Forbear your Addresses, and Court us no more,
For we will perform what the Deity swore:
But if you dare think of deserving our Charms,
Away with your Sheephooks, and take to your Arms;
Then Lawrels and Myrtles your Brows shall adorn,
When *Pan*, and his Son, and fair *Syrinx*, return.

Lyrics, except for their dramatic turns of dialogue, do not normally call attention to their shaping. Pace is largely the secret, but the rhetorical structuring takes place within a range of formal possibilities the good lyrist quietly exploits. Some of the most frequent possibilities are dialogue, shifts of voice, chronology (narrative, or presentation, or contrasting), logical formings (disjunction, entailment or apparent entailment, causal sequence, exemplification), various formal shapes repeated or inverted or varied, and—what is frequently thought of as most typical of lyric—association.[15] Grammatical forms and links (parallel structures, referents, conjunctions, and such) both express those rhetorical and logical possibilities, and add tissue and substance within and through themselves.

In "I feed a flame within" there is a nice joining of such forms. The first stanza presents, develops—defines —the nature of the flame, which the "I" feeds, and the nature of her relation to the flame. The correlative statements carry much of the weight of that definition. The second stanza offers a contrasting truth: the flame, intense, is hidden from the object of the flame.

49

Linking words are contrastive: "Yet" and "Not" and "But." The third stanza repeats and extends through apparent entailment ("Thus") and chronology ("while"). The fourth stanza moves forward to future time and finishes with a highly definitive balancing of qualities (the grammatical sign is "Nor"). The flame, the speaker, the loved one move into their relation through the help of such formal means. Resonant of feeling, and of finely fugitive shades of feeling as the poem is, the structure is not primarily associative.

"No no, poor suff'ring Heart" has a balanced (2-4-2) outward shape for the first stanza. The first two lines are an address to the heart, the next four are about the relationship between the heart and the "she," the last two are addressed to the "she." The second stanza is future tense, but not thereby narrative or even clearly chronological in forward motion. Four parallel statements convey the same doubleness: the "happy Minute" and the "Ages" which slide away. The happy minute is within the ages, the ages within the happy minute. Both are within the stationary, spatial room which Cupid guards. Time and Death and Change do depart, and the act of departure is in the future "now," the room, the happy minute. What happens is smoothly moving forward within stillness: the structure reflects the substance.

The Lady's Song, if less brilliant with metaphysical paradox, is as clean of order. The first stanza tells a story: the May-Day election and the refusal of the garland. The second stanza gives the reason for the refusal: that the garland should be refused within the span of time of the "While" in which Cupid waits and the " 'Till" for which he waits. The third stanza shifts in speaker from the singular Phillis to the plural Quire, and the "bright Beauties" order the suitors to leave them alone during the "While" until the " 'Till," the return (the new Restoration) which shall complete the circle of the poem and shall make possible a true May-Day, a granting of the suits.

These three songs demonstrate the variousness of Dryden's formal powers in that they are typical of his songs. In beauty and substance they are, however, exceptions.[16] Dryden, for all his skill, seldom avoids in his songs the limitations of Restoration taste and morality. "No no, poor suff'ring Heart," for all its beauty, still retains some traces of the taint. The lyrics were written mostly for plays and keyed to public taste. Insofar as they follow that taste they are flawed: brilliant expressions of an idea of love that does violence to the ideals which Dryden expressed in most of his criticism and poetry.

4

And English Oak:
The Heroic Quatrain

DRYDEN AT ONE time felt the heroic quatrain to be the most proper form for serious occasional poetry.[1] Harmonious and dignified, slow of motion and symmetrical of shape, it fits generalization and meditation.[2] The most famous example of it in English, Gray's *Elegy Written in a Country Churchyard*, is mostly dignified and generalized meditation.

The firmness of shape of the heroic quatrain restricts its use. The stanza is long enough to be felt as a whole, hence variety of verse paragraphing is next to impossible, though something like it can be attained by overflow between stanzas. The rhetorical shaping within a stanza can in varying degrees fit the metrical shape. To fit it too closely is to stiffen; not to fit it is to wander.

In narrative, the stanza is most appropriate when the action is explored by a mind that surveys moral meaning in history,[3] as does Dryden in his two uses of the form, the *Heroic Stanzas* in memory of Cromwell, and *Annus*

Mirabilis. The meditation often moves in the circuits of parallelism and antithesis. The rhymes make strong links, and the four lines have some tendency to echo meter by rhetoric, dividing into two pairs, parallel within each pair and between the pairs. Stanza 45 of *Annus Mirabilis* shows that arrangement in unusually complete form.

> He without fear a dangerous War pursues,
> Which without rashness he began before.
> As Honour made him first the danger choose,
> So still he makes it good on virtues score.[4]
> (vv. 177–80)

Lines 177 and 178 are parallel in words and thought; so are lines 179 and 180. Then the two pairs of line are parallel, line 179 explaining line 177 and line 180 explaining 178. Few stanzas fit the form so nearly; in fact this is the most extreme example in the two poems; and even here there is variety within the lines: for instance, the verbs, nouns, and prepositional phrases of parallel constructions stand at different places within respective lines. Still, the ground pattern is never far from mind or ear, and in both of Dryden's poems there is something sluggish and artificial, not quite manageable, in the variety of movement achieved. Such faults are strong inherent dangers of the form—witness *Gondibert;* their absence in Gray (and in some parts of Dryden's poems) prove that they are not necessary to it.

The *Heroic Stanzas* in memory of Cromwell is Dryden's first good poem. It is stiff-jointed; it is uneven; but the talent has ripened extraordinarily since the Hastings Elegy (in fact it would take something of clairvoyance—or hindsight—to find any talent to ripen in that poem). Dryden, if uncertainly, is finding the meaning of a poetic form.

The political question is not so easily put aside as some of his defenders would have it.[5] *Astraea Redux* does walk close on the heels of this example of the sort of hyperbolical praise which Dryden throughout his career was prone to scatter with a hand more politic than delicate. To say with Johnson that he changed with the nation is not much of a compliment to a man who took so harsh a view of the nation's fickleness. It is true, as Dryden's defenders have said, that the "breathing of the vein" of verse 48 is general rather than specific. Nothing in the context points to the beheading of Charles specifically; everything points to the war, the "bloodletting" in general. But it remains true, with a logical thump, that the general entails the specific, that *that* specific was most vividly in the nation's mind, and that —if Dryden meant to exclude it—his silence is at best pusillanimous. Nor does it quite do to say that Dryden always approved of strong government, of order over anarchy. For Dryden, in the rest of his political thought, approved of reasonably strong and legitimate government, a balance of powers which supported social order and individual freedom. That is finally what divine right means to Dryden: the divine right of magistracy. Either a government is founded in right, in natural law (which to a theist means divine right, divine law), or all governments rule by force or fraud. That is a hard disjunction, and one that Dryden understood more intelligently than many modern liberals and conservatives. Dryden felt this so strongly that he could, in "The Lady's Song," call for revolution (with at least romantic seriousness: he meant what he said even if he wasn't collecting guns) when he felt that the rightful ruler had been deposed. Strong government without right, even though orderly, is tyranny and usurpation, and Dryden is to call **Cromwell** a usurper in *Annus Mirabilis* (v. 40).

The "singular and happy delicacy" of which **Scott** speaks and the California editors approve,[6] of not saying anything against the Royalists, can be read as more canny than noble. To be sure, it does not have to be read so; Dryden could genuinely approve much about Cromwell; he does say much which fits his permanent political ideas; the praise is largely judicious; and there may be some hints, which I shall develop shortly, of doubleness of attitude toward Cromwell. While I am entirely persuaded that Dryden after 1660 cannot justly be called turncoat or time-server in politics or religion, I am less persuaded for 1659 to 1660. The stanzas are not so damning as his enemies claimed; and he may have simply changed his mind. But the "may" remains; and there is no "may" to it that he would have been happier in later years if this poem had not been around.

The structure of the *Heroic Stanzas* is sound, if a little dull. The poem suffers from the extrinsic deliberateness of expected design. The design is not exactly, in Coleridge's meaning, "mechanic," since it is highly natural ("organic") to the kind: a funeral panegyric of a man of action whose life was of political and religious importance in a nation's life. Such a form calls for meditation, preparation, praise, narration, and a final signature conveying the moral and religious meaning of the career. The structure of the poem is roughly as follows:

Stanzas 1–4 It is time to mourn, publicly
Stanza 5 How shall I begin to draw his praise?

Though the outward structure is firm, the poem is off in timing. The movement is sluggish and one feels no sense of building toward and into a height and untying of action. Partly this comes from the stanza's tendency to curtail and to overshape motion, partly from the poet's apprentice skill. There is also a lack of vibrant continuity and intermingling of the imagery. In the brilliant and varied imagery of some of Dryden's best poetry, *Absalom and Achitophel*, *The Medal*, *Mac Flecknoe*, the Anne Killigrew Ode, the images shine together and work the surface toward unity, even as in their meanings they move on thematic centerings. Here one senses the deliberate ornamentation of prior designs. The ornaments, whether noble or clumsy, remain isolated from each other.

The sense of meditative stasis outdraws the sense of motion. "His Name a great example *stands* to show" (v. 146, emphasis mine). Stanza 13 proves something of the form by metrically contradicting itself (emphasis his).

Swift and resistless through the Land he past
Like that bold *Greek* who did the East subdue;

> And made to battails such Heroick haste
> As if on wings of victory he flew.
>
> (vv. 49–52)

The wings are hardly swift; the verbs stick at line ends; they don't fly.[7] Yet there is an eloquence about the stanza. The heroes stand, in extratemporal space.

The poem has its successes and, compared to the more erratic *Annus Mirabilis*, comparatively few failures. The best of it approaches the later Dryden. Stanza 6 begins well and ends very well:

> His *Grandeur* he deriv'd from Heav'n alone.
> For he was great e're Fortune made him so;
> And Warr's like mists that rise against the Sunne
> Made him but greater seem, not greater grow.
>
> (vv. 21–24)

Not only is the image a sound one, with some perhaps accidental but illuminating metaphysical resonance (war as evil, evil as privation), but he has the accents of the stanza exactly timed. *"Grandeur"* and "Heav'n" and "Fortune" touch together; they suborder and locate the "great" of verse 22. The third verse carries the ground beat, and in the fourth the two *greater*'s, which are one in meaning, stand off as predominant from the rest and equal in accent. Dryden is learning what meter has to say.

Stanza 11 puts three genuine and percipient antitheses (within the second, third, and fourth verses) through a nice shifting of places. The "sticklers" (umpires) is a good metaphor, and the stanza states permanent truth with the ring of definition which, the secret once learned, Dryden was not to forget.

> Our former Cheifs like sticklers of the Warre
> First sought t' inflame the Parties, then to poise;
> The quarrell lov'd, but did the cause abhorre,
> And did not strike to hurt but make a noise.
>
> (vv. 41–44)

Stanza 12 (alas for Dryden later!) is one of the best turned, again handling the twoness with harmonious change.

> Warre our consumption was their gainfull trade,
> We inward bled whilst they prolong'd our pain:
> He fought to end the fighting, and assaid
> To stanch the blood by breathing of the vein.
>
> (vv. 45–48)

The first line of the stanza brilliantly handles rhetorical accent.[8] The stress which meaning requires for "our" and "their" pushes the respective feet just beyond spondees, so that iamb and trochee become reversed. That is, without rhetorical stress the lines scan thus:

> | Warre   our | consump | tion   was | their   gain | full
> trade | t i *i* i i

With rhetorical stress:

> | Warre our | consumption was | their gain | full trade
>   *i*   T

In the next line rhetorical stress on *we* and *they* reinforces the movement.

> | We   in | ward   bled | whilst   they | prolong'd | our
> pain | t i i i i

58

The result is a concentrated and noble scorn inflected in the "their" and "they," which prepares for the reinforced "He" (Cromwell) and the good metaphor and curiously quiet, breathing sound of "breathing of the vein."

Stanza 23 jokes with "light" and heavy ("grave"), and with the balancing potentialities of the form itself. Stanzas 24, 26, and 37 realize especially well the dignified potentialities of the form.

Repeatedly, tones cross the panegyric. The last half of stanza 7 ("Nor was his Vertue poyson'd *soon* as born / With the *too early* thoughts of being King" [emphasis mine]) virtually begs to be unfolded into a sneer: *"that* sort of nasty ambition came later." In stanza 8, Cromwell is the ancient servant of a coy and hard whore, Fortune, and he is contrasted with Pompey (Who is he to succeed at an age when the great Pompey failed?). Dryden had a penchant for coarsening traditional metaphors, and any comparison may backfire. At the very best, though, it is an unfortunate stanza. The "private" of stanza 9, verse 1 sounds like a harsh pun, which makes Cromwell secretly designing as well as not-yet-famous. Even if that ambiguity is not intended, stanza 10, especially its first verse ("And yet *Dominion* was not his Designe") sounds more like a contradiction than a qualification to stanza 9. Cromwell ends up sounding as though he were scheming. If the "blessing" of stanza 10, line 2 (verse 38) is a sarcasm ("We owe that blessing not to him but Heaven"), the "Rewards" of line 4 (verse 40) of the same stanza ("Rewards that lesse to him than us were given") comes to mean God's punishment for the willful refusal of just obedience, a meaning very much in keeping with Dryden's later views and rhetorical habits. A hypersuspicious mind might worry a little about stanza 19 where, to reach the "Sov'raign Gold" of Cromwell's nature, the reader is directed "downward." It is hard even for the context in stanza 20 to make the "close *Intrigues*" sound like a compliment. In stanza 25, Cromwell is compared to an alchemist making a secret and illicit "brew," not an encouraging comparison.

Most of the praise is praise, and I do not wish to cultivate another crop of ambiguities, especially imaginary ones, but there are enough of such passages to puzzle. I suggest that perhaps they express some dimly recognized reluctance at the subject, a native tendency to satire growing a little wild, and a less than entirely professional skill at managing the complexities of his topics and techniques.

Annus Mirabilis, a more ambitious example of the form, is a great and shockingly bad poem, and I am uncertain how to assess the balance. The truth lies somewhere between Macaulay's assessment that the poem "seems to be the work of a man who could never, by any possibility, write poetry" [9] and the view of the California editors, who find, with only tucked-away qualification, almost all admirable, and even bring themselves to admire, as "grim irony" such passages as "The wild waves master'd him, and suck'd him in, / And smiling Eddies dimpled on the Main" (vv. 375–76). Mixing the pretty and grim is Ovidian, but being too pretty is coy. The poem is a close contemporary of *An Essay of Dramatic Poesy*, in which the style is consistently brilliant. In prose, a master; in verse, a bungling apprentice of genius, a combination so far as I know unique in

English or American letters, at least for a writer who was to go on to become a master of the higher art. Even that simplifies, for the apprentice is at times not only bungling but incompetent, and the same "apprentice" is, off and on, a master poet. The shaping is not entirely satisfactory, though the order is "logically" clear and adequate enough: action in relation to meditation and cumulative political-religious themes. As in the Cromwell elegy, the timing is off and the movement sluggish. The bragged-on use [10] of the classical sources is mostly servile and gawky imitation. The "machines" (angels) are, with rare exceptions, preposterous. Angels and mercantilism are hard to blend poetically, though I no more than Dryden know any solid reason why they might not join. In historical sections of *Paradise Lost,* such topics do. In general, the supernatural moves bluntly athwart the historical, though the ghosts fare better than the angels, and some providential turns carry felt themes. Many similes are dragged in by labor only to gasp their stumbling last; and the outlandish passages of the sorts remarked by critics from Johnson to Miner are if anything more frequent than those critics have said. I find something to laugh at, or wince at, in at least these stanzas: 15, 16, 59, 79, 94 (fourth verse), 98 (fourth verse), 155, 164 (fourth verse), 184, 221, 224, 232, 261, 271, 272, 281.

The question is not merely of a period style no longer available. It is of period styles and preperiod styles and influences (Virgil, Ovid, Cowley, Lucretius, painting, the metaphysical, the baroque, the comic, the scientific, the nautical, Lucan, the Bible).[11] It is a matter of his marshaling his riches, making his scholarship beautifully his own. In the best later poems, he does. Here he does sometimes.

Yet for all that, *Annus Mirabilis* has probably been underrated. The flaws have blinded eyes to high virtues of thought, expression, imagery, versification. The albatross waddles across the deck to take some lovely flights. And, as thematic realizations, the poem is rich and wise.

A special note of British gallantry which one can find across centuries from Shakespeare to the Cavalier poets to Kipling, and to some World War II poets,[12] is sounded in several passages:

> His wounded men he first sends off to shore:
>   (Never, till now, unwilling to obey.)
>   (Stanza 74, vv. 293–94)

> Yet, like an *English* Gen'ral will I die,
>   And all the Ocean make my spatious grave.
> Women and Cowards on the Land may lie,
>   The Sea's a Tomb that's proper for the brave.
>   (Stanza 101, vv. 401–404)

> With roomy decks, her Guns of mighty strength,
>   (Whose low-laid mouthes each mounting billow
>   laves:)
> Deep in her draught, and warlike in her length,
>   She seems a Sea-wasp flying on the waves.
>   (Stanza 153, vv. 609–12)

> Thousands were there in darker fame that dwell,
>   Whose deeds some nobler Poem shall adorn:
> And, though to me unknown, they, sure, fought well,
>   Whom *Rupert* led, and who were *British* born.
>   (Stanza 176, vv. 701–704)

Though there are more flaws than in the Cromwell poem, there is also a better sense of what the form may do. Dryden has learned to count "two" in a higher number of ways. In stanza 10 the King's thoughts balance, in a Latin manner: [13] "This saw our King; and long within his breast / His pensive counsels ballanc'd too and fro" (verses 37–38). Stanza 12 talks out the balance the stanza form presents.

> The loss and gain each fatally were great;
> And still his Subjects call'd aloud for war:
> But peaceful Kings o'r martial people set,
> Each others poize and counter-ballance are.
> (vv. 45–48)

The poise and counterbalance appear in three different sets of parallel terms, each placed and touched differently: loss and gain, subjects and kings, poise and counterbalance.

Holland and England are two. The leaders, Albermarle and Rupert, then Charles and James, are two. War and fire are two. Providence and history appear two, make one. The verse form is two at least twice. Dryden works the doublenesses skillfully.

Slowness crosses the narration and becomes its virtue.

> With them no riotous pomp, nor *Asian* train,
> T' infect a Navy with their gawdy fears:
> To make slow fights, and victories but vain;
> But war, severely, like it self, appears.
> (Stanza 52, vv. 205–208)

The third line forces a slow balance of itself. The fourth line is extraordinary: the ultimate likeness is identity, it steps forth to metaphysical plainness. Thus, truly, war. Yet it is not quite an identity either, since it is myth (person, personification, apotheosis) and only-too-factual fact. Is Poseidon the sea? He has a blue beard.[14] Is war war? Yes, its present similitude.[15] The scansion of the line is five iambs; the shape is iamb, amphibrach, anapest, iamb; and the change and stillness enforce and present the severity of the verse.

Stanzas 61 and 62 are admirably Drydenian in their nobility, their grace of movement, the plain and strong dignity in the similes of the Virgilian oak and the steeple, and funnily, irritatingly Drydenian in the joke hidden in the eloquence (that the Duke's breeches were shot off).[16]

> Our dreaded Admiral from far they threat,
> Whose batter'd rigging their whole war receives.
> All bare, like some old Oak which tempests beat,
> He stands, and sees below his scatter'd leaves.
>
> *Heroes* of old, when wounded, shelter sought,
> But he, who meets all danger with disdain,
> Ev'n in their face his ship to Anchor brought,
> And Steeple high stood propt upon the Main.
>
> (vv. 241–48)

Stanzas 68–71 are, as Johnson said, among the "fairest flowers" of our poetry, and the fourth verse of stanza 69 shows that Dryden had already learned the magic in quantity and in liquid slowness: the poignance and strangeness of that verse and of the stanzas are qualities of Dryden, though not the qualities most often mentioned by his critics. Several of Dryden's favorite images meet in somber power in the stanzas: moonlight, flame, darkness, the sea, an enchanted ground.

> The night comes on, we, eager to pursue
> The Combat still, and they asham'd to leave:
> Till the last streaks of dying day withdrew,
> And doubtful Moon-light did our rage deceive.
>
> In th' *English* Fleet each ship resounds with joy,
> And loud applause of their great Leader's fame.
> In fiery dreams the *Dutch* they still destroy,
> And, slumbring, smile at the imagin'd flame.
>
> Not so the *Holland* Fleet, who tir'd and done,
> Stretch'd on their decks like weary Oxen lie:
> Faint sweats all down their mighty members run,
> (Vast bulks which little souls but ill supply.)
>
> In dreams they fearful precipices tread,
> Or, shipwrack'd, labour to some distant shore:
> Or in dark Churches walk among the dead:
> They wake with horrour, & dare sleep no more.
>
> (vv. 269–84)

Almost equally strange, and almost equally beautiful is stanza 102, quiet of war's evil and presence.[17] Ships burn in war at night, and Dryden's fires travel with them.

> Restless he pass'd the remnants of the night,
> Till the fresh air proclaim'd the morning nigh,
> And burning ships, the Martyrs of the fight,
> With paler fires beheld the Eastern sky.
>
> (vv. 405–408)

The lights that vary in the early air of verse 408 reflect the "becalmed floud" of moonlight in stanza 99 and the ray of the sun's "Star" in stanza 100.

The first half of stanza 120 has been rightly praised. The mimesis of the second line is as thickly of the mouth as of the ear. The last two lines are almost as good, the

65

fourth line having a tongued precision of meaning which enters and enforces the wry and stark personification.

> His presence soon blows up the kindling fight,
>   And his loud Guns speak thick like angry men:
> It seem'd as slaughter had been breath'd all night,
>   And death new pointed his dull dart agen.
> (vv. 477–80)

Stanza 256 is tender and ghostly in quality and has the distinction of having made possible one of the most haunting moments in Gray's elegy.

> Those who have none sit round where once it was,
>   And with full eyes each wonted room require:
> Haunting the yet warm ashes of the place,
>   As murder'd men walk where they did expire.
> (vv. 1021–24)

> On some fond breast the parting soul relies,
> Some pious drops the closing eye requires;
> Ev'n from the tomb the voice of Nature cries,
> Ev'n in our Ashes live their wonted Fires.
> (vv. 89–92 of Gray's *Elegy*) [18]

The Apostrophe to the Royal Society (stanzas 165 and 166) is wise with a passion and insight too often forgotten in decades and centuries to come.

> This I fore-tel, from your auspicious care,
>   Who great in search of God and Nature grow:
> Who best your wise Creator's praise declare,
>   Since best to praise his works is best to know.

> O truly Royal! who behold the Law,
>   And rule of beings in your Makers mind,

> And then, like Limbecks, rich Idea's draw,
> To fit the levell'd use of humane kind.
>
> (vv. 657–64)

Verse 660 has a fascinating twoness, at last oneness, of meaning. It means primarily that the best praise for God's creation is achieving true scientific knowledge of it, but it also can mean the Wordsworthian vision: to encounter in praise the lovely waters and splendid sun and moonlight of God's creation is itself the best knowledge.[19] The metaphorical complexity of verse 658 helps support that meaning, as does the "auspicious" of verse 657 which suggests that God's prevenient grace goes before the knowledge of his works. Through his providential care his creation may be known and praised, a meaning that fits the central theme of the poem.

The introduction of Charles' prayer ends with one of the poem's poorest stanzas, 261. The prayer itself is beautiful, especially stanzas 262–65. If Charles and the London populace had both heeded, some exciting English history might not have happened (and heaven had wanted one immortal song).

Some of the best of the poem's imagery is simple, providential, and biblical, notably in stanzas 212 and 253. One line is literal, yet wears the dignity of Dryden's best royalist metaphors: "Now day appears, and with the day the King" (v. 949). One of the best stanzas has in it, half hidden, another example of one of Dryden's favorite images, enchanted ground.[20]

> Our King this more then natural change beholds;
> With sober joy his heart and eyes abound:

67

> To the All-good his lifted hands he folds,
> And thanks him low on his redeemed ground.
>
> (Stanza 283, vv. 1129–32)

It is sad but I fear not untypical that this is in response to what is probably the poem's champion absurdity: God's fire-extinguisher.

Many other passages are admirable. One of the most important gives the central providential vision of the poem,[21] the central royalist analogy, and a good if accidental comment on the poem itself.

> As those who unripe veins in Mines explore,
> On the rich bed again the warm turf lay,
> Till time digests the yet imperfect Ore,
> And know it will be Gold another day:
>
> So looks our Monarch on this early fight,
> Th' essay, and rudiments of great success,
> Which all-maturing time must bring to light,
> While he, like Heav'n, does each days labour bless.
>
> Heav'n ended not the first or second day,
> Yet each was perfect to the work design'd:
> God and Kings work, when they their work survey,
> And passive aptness in all subjects find.
>
> (Stanzas 139–41, vv. 553–64)

One can hardly call a poem with so many weak moments a success but one cannot call a poem a failure which expresses coherently a high vision, and which has many beautiful passages. Anything like a fair final judgment is hard to come at. Perhaps it is not the point. For there are the other forms that Dryden did cultivate, most especially, of course, the heroic couplet.

5

Oh Narrow Circle:
The Heroic Couplet

THE COUPLET HAS two major and basic virtues: it provides a very firm metrical and rhetorical norm; unlike poems in stanzas, it allows great flexibility, both within a couplet and in forward motion through couplets. Within a couplet, variation can be achieved by counterpatterning and by manipulations of phrasing, accent, pauses, speed, and quantity. Even though a couplet is closed, the mind and ear are not compelled to stop short at the end of every second verse. Couplets may combine in paragraphs of many lengths.

The general characteristics of the heroic couplet as used by Dryden are well known.[1] The couplet is usually closed (end-stopped after the second line). The number of syllables in masculine lines is constant (except for substitution of hexameters); that is, Dryden practically never uses a trisyllabic foot.[2] Feminine lines are rare. Truncation is very rare, if not nonexistent. He allows the

Alexandrine, the fourteener (rarely), and the triplet as variations.[3] He normally avoids enjambment; his rhymes (often near rhymes) tend to be strongly stressed; a pause occurs after most verses, though a pause at the end of the first verse may be light. Disyllabic substitutions occur, especially in the first place or after a pause. Alliteration and other sound-links are frequent, and often bind sense and motion, as does metrical parallelism. Monosyllabic verses are not common.[4] Euphony is sought, except when harshness is proper to mood or meaning. Medial pauses occur often enough to set up counterpatterns. However, variation of phrase-ends in degree (from a phrase-end [5] with no real pause to very heavy pauses marked by periods or semicolons) as well as in placing within the line, is a major method of variation.

Perhaps in this summary the strength of the norm has been more apparent than the modes of variation. Yet Dryden's couplet is capable of great variety within the fixed frame. It has extraordinary power, suppleness, and range. It obeys the fundamental rule of good metrics: that the norm never be lost, yet the variations never be arithmetically simple or predictable.

> He moves excentric, like a wandering star,
> Whose motion's just, though 'tis not regular.[6]

That couplet nicely illustrates its meaning. The first verse displays one of Dryden's chief counterpatterns, which I shall refer to at times as a "secondary norm," a medial phrase-end with accents on either side approximately balanced with each other. The pause is after the fifth syllable, and the lightness of the technically accented sixth syllable leaves two strong accents on either side of the pause. Even this verse is a little "excentric." The slight anapestic-like leap in the second half-verse has no counterpart in the first half-verse (when Dryden wants a very regular verse to close a passage, he often writes a balanced hexameter). In the second verse of the couplet the variation from such a pattern is striking: i i | *t* i i.

$5 - 1 = 4$. $2 + 2 = 4$. $2 = 2$. What my arithmetic lacks in originality or complexity it may make up in metrical relevance. That is, there are five technical accents in almost all iambic pentameters (spondees or pyrrhics can throw the count off). If one of those five stresses is weak (technically stressed by the principle of relative accent because stronger than the other syllable in the foot, but distinctly lighter than the other stressed syllables in the verse), there are four strong accents. But four can balance out two against two, and does so when there is any medial pause or phrase-end. Since, however, the two strong stresses in each half-line can come at different places in different lines, and since a medial pause or phrase-end can come after syllable four, five, or six, nearly balanced lines offer a variety of shapes which can play against each other, as in a couplet of *Absalom and Achitophel* which shows one of Dryden's favorite images, the circle, at its best and metaphysically most resonant.

> Oh Narrow Circle, but of Pow'r Divine,
> Scanted in Space, but perfect in thy Line!
> (vv. 838–39)

The balancing of stressed syllables goes 2 4 | 8 10; 1 4 | 6 10 in the two verses, the medial pause shifting from after the fifth syllable to after the fourth. By a happy accident, the couplet, praising Barzillai's son (who died early), speaks with its own authority about the heroic couplet.

The pattern of balance within a verse (like the frequent balances that work between the two verses) is very obviously proper to twoness of meaning: parallelism, antithesis. Yet it is easy to overrate their importance in Dryden's poetry. Even George Williamson, who finds in parallelism and antithesis the basic rhetoric of the tradition of the neoclassic heroic couplet, says that Dryden as often departs from that tradition as supports it.[7] In the couplet quoted above, the metrically balanced verse ("He moves excentric, like a wandering star") is not antithetical, but the metrically unbalanced verse ("Whose motion's just, though 'tis not regular") is. In general, Dryden gains a freedom beyond his fellows.

That freedom is compatible with the strong norms of the couplet. Metrical stress and parallelism emphasize the fact that words stressed and paralleled *are* related. The relations so pointed up may be almost any kind of relations—akin, unlike, oblique.

The variations that Dryden uses are several, and give a range of freedom within the strong frame. He allows the substitution of disyllabic feet, but that freedom is less important than the freedom gained by the skillful changes of degree of accent within the regular iambic foot. Unaccented syllables range in stress from very light to fairly strong, accented syllables range from fairly light to extremely heavy. Quantity is perfectly free: it may reinforce or cross the accentual pattern; it may qualify or strengthen meanings. Phrase-ends are varied in placing and length: they are found after any syllable in the verse (though most commonly after the fifth and the tenth syllables); they may vary from short to long. Words that are in themselves trochees or dactyls at times create a slight counterrhythm to the normally rising cadency. Relations between half-verses, verses, and the couplet are very diverse, and like most of the other metrical variations, can fit many kinds of meaning. Dryden's couplets are seldom dull to an ear that has learned their ways.

Nor are those ways, despite the widespread opinion of critics,[8] chiefly the ways of statement, epigram and satire. Dryden's couplets are properly responsive to narrative, to dramatic conflict, to the tender perception of natural beauty.

To achieve such responsiveness, the heroic couplet must achieve freedom of verse paragraphing without violating its basic norms. In fact, without some verse paragraphing each couplet would be simply a separate unit, and a poem in couplets could have no unity. Yet the closed couplet does have a tendency to establish a strong boundary which neither sense nor rhythm can easily cross.

Dryden crosses that divide with an ease that is extraordinary, even in his Prologues and Epilogues, which, comprised often of disrelated remarks, have less need of verse paragraphing than do other genres. A minor form that Dryden thoroughly mastered, the prologue-epilogue serves well to begin showing the ways in which Dryden handles the heroic couplet.

The Prologue to *All for Love* is a typical and excellent example. I indicate with a series of brackets the smaller and larger metrical and rhetorical "paragraphs."

What Flocks of Critiques hover here to day,
As Vultures wait on Armies for their Prey,
All gaping for the Carcass of a Play!
With Croaking Notes they bode some dire event;
And follow dying Poets by the scent.   5

Ours gives himself for gone; y'have watch'd your time!
He fights this day unarm'd; without his Rhyme.
And brings a Tale which often has been told;
As sad as *Dido*'s; and almost as old.

His Heroe, whom you Wits his Bully call,   10
Bates of his mettle; and scarce rants at all:
He's somewhat lewd; but a well-meaning mind;
Weeps much; fights little; but is wond'rous kind.
In short, a Pattern, and Companion fit,
For all the keeping Tonyes of the Pit.   15

I cou'd name more: A Wife, and Mistress too;
Both (to be plain) too good for most of you:
The Wife well-natur'd, and the Mistress true.

 Now, Poets, if your fame has been his care;
Allow him all the candour you can spare.   20
A brave Man scorns to quarrel once a day;
Like Hectors, in at every petty fray.

Let those find fault whose Wit's so very small,
They've need to show that they can think at all:
Errours like Straws upon the surface flow;   25
He who would search for Pearls must dive below.
Fops may have leave to level all they can;
As Pigmies wou'd be glad to lopp a Man.
Half-Wits are Fleas; so little and so light;
We scarce cou'd know they live, but that they bite. 30

But, as the Rich, when tir'd with daily Feasts,
For change, become their next poor Tenants Ghests;
Drink hearty Draughts of Ale, from plain brown Bowls,
And snatch the homely Rasher from the Coals:
So you, retiring from much better Cheer,   35
For once, may venture to do penance here.
And since that plenteous Autumn now is past,
Whose Grapes and Peaches have Indulg'd your taste,
Take in good part from our poor Poets boord,
Such rivell'd Fruits as Winter can afford.   40

The verse paragraphing, of course, permits some choice and some debate, but the larger sections are well marked, and the transitions from section to section are smooth, especially considering the several tasks the poet performs. Apology, parody, hectoring, and flattery interlace with commentary on literature and human affairs in general. Many grammatical links (pronouns, conjunctions, sentence modifiers) smooth the transitions, but the metrical linkage is important too. Dryden, by various devices, holds back full relief from the ear until the ends of sections. Triplets end sections, the third rhyme being strongly felt. Balanced verses likewise close out sections, notably verses 9, 18, and 36.

Metrical parallelism does some striking service. In verses 2 and 3, which conclude an analogy strong in contempt, metrics and wording alike find their parallels. The following (unusual) marking shows the stronger accents in each line and the relations of words to corresponding words and of phrases to corresponding phrases.

> As Vultures || wait on Armies || for their Prey,
>
> All gaping || for the Carcass || of a Play!

The closeness of the analogy is supported by the virtual identity of sound pattern.

In verses 25–30 the three couplets, each tightly closed and epigrammatic, enforce their parallelism (and consequently strengthen the attack) by the placing of phrase-ends: in each couplet, the main phrase-end in the first verse is after the fourth syllable, the main phrase-end in the second verse after the sixth syllable. Against such regularity of cadency, the verses that follow, especially verses 31–34, are felt as extremely varied and free. I do not know whether there is any specific propriety of metrics to meaning within those lines, but at least the change in cadency fits the change from direct attack to a modest cheerfulness.

Variety in phrasing throughout the poem is considerable, both in the placing of phrase-ends and in the degree of separation between successive phrases. Nevertheless, phrase-ends stay near enough to the center so that a phrase-end after any of the first three syllables is felt as a departure from the norm. Of the eight main phrase-ends that come early in the verse, four (in verse 10, after syllable 3; verse 19, after syllables 1 and 3; verse 31, after syllable 1) introduce new passages. Each of these phrase-ends reflects the clear contrast shown by the transitional words. Another phrase-end that comes early in a verse (verse 22, after syllable 3) gives strong emphasis. It is, largely, the control of metrical transition, parallelism and variation that makes the Prologue not a series of disjointed remarks, but a poem.

Dryden's skill in passing from norm to variation, from section to section, from sound to meaning, is clearly at work in more serious genres. Some techniques appear, with slight changes, in different genres; some are restricted to special effects.

In *Mac Flecknoe*, for instance, we again find phrase-ends tending toward the center of the verse, balanced verses closing passages; we also find something new: a preponderance of very heavy accent, as in these verses:

> Nor let false friends seduce thy mind to fame,
> By arrogating *Johnson's* Hostile name.

Let Father *Fleckno* fire thy mind with praise,
And Uncle *Ogleby* thy envy raise.
Thou art my blood, where *Johnson* has no part;
What share have we in Nature or in Art?

(vv. 171–76)

The seven accents in the first verse, the powerful "arrogating," the alliteration of "Father *Fleckno* fire" that stresses among other things the contrast with Ben Jonson, the vocal ugliness of "*Ogleby*" intensified by the "Uncle" that marks a kinship and issue of dullness, the phrasing and stress of verse 176 that makes us attend to the standards of the poem (the nature and art from which Shadwell and his kind are excluded)—all these strengthen the realization of what Shadwell is and what he is not. They contribute to the metaphysics of satire.[9]

The verses that immediately follow are a nice study in climactic parallelism:

Where did his wit on learning fix a brand,
And rail at Arts he did not understand?
Where made he love in Prince *Nicander's* vein,
Or swept the dust in *Psyche's* humble strain?
Where sold he Bargains, Whip-stitch, kiss my Arse,
Promis'd a Play and dwindled to a Farce?

(vv. 177–82)

The first two verses are strong in accent and steady in forward progress. The next two are very closely parallel through the sixth syllable in meter, syntax, and word-syllable relations. There is enough variation after the sixth syllable to support the comic antithesis between Shadwell's heroic and humble styles (which, as the parallelism suggests, come to the same dullness), and to

77

provide a real antithesis between Shadwell and Ben Jonson. The fifth verse begins with a half-verse and a medial pause, finishes in exact iambics but inelegant sound and vulgar meaning offered as typical of Shadwell's style, providing a contrast with the first half-verse and an even greater contrast with the euphonious and nicely balanced verse that completes the couplet. The contrast judges Shadwell's style. The last verse quoted (which scans t i | i i i), with its balance of strong accents enclosing light syllables on each side of the phrase-end, exhibits with deadly emphasis the "promise" and failure of Shadwell's plays.

Strong accentuation is a keynote of the poem. For instance, more than ten verses of the next-to-last section (vv. 171–210) have six or more strongly accented syllables, some of which are very heavy. Quietness comes as a variation at the close.

> And down they sent the yet declaiming Bard.
> Sinking he left his Drugget robe behind,
> Born upwards by a subterranean wind.
> The Mantle fell to the young Prophet's part,
> With double portion of his Father's Art.
>
> (vv. 213–17)

The first verse is forcible, ends a passage. Fleckno's departure, and its aftermath, are quieter. The perturbation of "Born upwards by a subterranean wind" comes not from heavy accentuation but from the varying motion of the first three syllables and the last seven. The verse ends quietly, and the poem ends with simple, if mock, dignity, the last verse resolving to a near-perfect balance.

Less good-natured, less humorous, and less smooth,

but no less potent, are Dryden's translations of Juvenal, among the best translations he ever made. The First Satire opens in full angry flight:

> Still shall I hear, and never quit the Score,
> Stun'd with hoarse *Codrus Theseid,* o're and o're?
> Shall this Man's Elegies and t'others Play
> Unpunish'd Murther a long Summer's day?
> Huge *Telephus,* a formidable page,   5
> Cries Vengeance; and *Orestes* bulky rage
> Unsatisfy'd with Margins closely writ,
> Foams o're the Covers, and not finish'd yet.
> No Man can take a more familiar note
> Of his own Home, than I of *Vulcan's* Grott,   10
> Or *Mars his Grove,* or hollow winds that blow
> From *Ætna's* top, or tortur'd Ghosts below.
> I know by rote the Fam'd Exploits of *Greece;*
> The Centaurs fury, and the Golden Fleece;
> Through the thick shades th' Eternal Scribler
>   bauls;   15
> And shakes the Statues on their Pedestals.

Nowhere in our poetry is the potential awkwardness of English (and of some classical names) put to better use. Consonant heaped on consonant and the clustering of thick accents combine formidably in such phrases as "hoarse *Codrus Theseid,*" "Unpunish'd Murther," and "a formidable page." The word "Foams" gains power from its metrical prominence (it is in a reversed foot and followed by light syllables) and from the heavy quantity that contrasts with the last syllables of the preceding verse, as well as from the grandiose accuracy of the metaphor. In verse 15, it is metrical emphasis as much as meaning that condemns the "Eternal Scribler" to the "thick shades." Saintsbury said, correctly, that Dryden

79

always attacks from above.[10] Here he drops very heavy weights on the offending heads.

Dryden's couplets also serve serious purposes well, as in one of the greatest and most highly admired passages from *The Hind and the Panther,* The First Part:

> What weight of antient witness can prevail
> If private reason hold the publick scale?
> But, gratious God, how well dost thou provide
> For erring judgments an unerring Guide!   65
> Thy throne is darkness in th' abyss of light,
> A blaze of glory that forbids the sight;
> O teach me to believe Thee thus conceal'd,
> And search no farther than thy self reveal'd;
> But her alone for my Directour take   70
> Whom thou hast promis'd never to forsake!
> My thoughtless youth was wing'd with vain desires,
> My manhood, long misled by wandring fires,
> Follow'd false lights; and when their glimps was gone,
> My pride struck out new sparkles of her own.   75
> Such was I, such by nature still I am,
> Be thine the glory, and be mine the shame.
> Good life be now my task: my doubts are done,
> (What more could fright my faith, than Three in One?)
> Can I believe eternal God could lye   80
> Disguis'd in mortal mold and infancy?
> That the great maker of the world could dye?
> And after that, trust my imperfect sense
> Which calls in question his omnipotence?
> Can I my reason to my faith compell,   85
> And shall my sight, and touch, and taste rebell?
> Superiour faculties are set aside,
> Shall their subservient organs be my guide?
> Then let the moon usurp the rule of day,
> And winking tapers shew the sun his way;   90

> For what my senses can themselves perceive
> I need no revelation to believe.
> Can they who say the Host should be descry'd
> By sense, define a body glorify'd?
> Impassible, and penetrating parts?   95
> Let them declare by what mysterious arts
> He shot that body through th' opposing might
> Of bolts and barrs impervious to the light,
> And stood before his train confess'd in open sight.

The passage glows with exaltation, yet maintains firm control and balance. The balance appears in the verse paragraphing: the paragraphs close, amost without fail, with a balanced line. Assuming that verse paragraphs close at verses 65, 67, 71, 75, 77, 84, 92, and 99, one finds that most of the closing lines are balanced. Verse 99 is a hexameter with three accents on either side of the caesura. In verse 71, which has a light accent in the fourth foot, there are two heavy accents on either side of the medial phrase-end (after the fifth syllable). Verses 65, 67, and 77 fit the most basic of balanced patterns: i i *i* i i with a pause after the fifth syllable. The resolving effect of such verses is nowhere better shown than in this couplet, verses 64–65:

> But, gratious God, how well dost thou provide
> For erring judgments an unerring Guide!

The last verse, by setting man's weakness in the first half-verse against the church's infallibility in the second, resolves the mind. The metrics support the resolution of the spiritual and intellectual problem. The next two verses, in imagery two of the most remarkable that Dryden ever wrote, are balanced with awesome weight:

| Thy throne | is dark | ness || in | th' abyss | of light, |

             i i *i* i i

| A blaze | of glo | ry || that | forbids | the sight |

             i i *i* i i

The superb music of verses 72–77 is largely in the harmonious variation of pause and phrasing, resolved by the secondary norm, very slow and very balanced, of

| Be thine | the glo | ry, || and | be mine | the shame. |

             i i *i* i i

The strong surge and countersurge of the rhetorical questions and answers (verses 79–88) manifest the strength of his feeling that his doubts were finished. The triumphant answer of verses 89–92 sets off balanced against unbroken lines, the two norms of the couplet.

| Then let | the   moon || usurp | the rule | of   day, |

             i i i i i

| And wink | ing tap | ers || shew | the sun | his way; |

             i i *i* i i

| For   what | my   sens | es || can | themselves | perceive |

             i i *i* i i

| I need | no rev | ela | tion to | believe. | i i i *i* i

                                   (vv. 89–92)

Verses 89 and 90 show the contrast very exactly, verse 89 fitting the basic motion of iambic pentameter about as nearly as a verse can, quantity and isochronism reinforcing the stress pattern, verse 90 balancing two strong accents on either side of the medial pause. Verse 91 is likewise balanced, and verse 92 turns back toward, though not quite to, the basic norm. The two balanced verses alter from each other at the heart of the line. So do the normative lines. The "shew" of verse 90 is stronger than the "can" of verse 91, the "surp" of verse 89 than the "la" of verse 92. The patterning and counterpatterning fulfill the demands of the ear and mind.

The purpose of the hexameter in Dryden is often to express the surging of passion, and sometimes to simulate it when it is not present. The passion needs no simulation here: verse 99, like its subject and like the emotion with which it is charged, bursts powerfully beyond the normal scheme of things.

Dryden creates the same effect at the end of an even more famous passage, the opening of *Religio Laici*.

> Dim, as the borrow'd beams of Moon and Stars
> To *lonely, weary, wandring* Travellers,
> Is *Reason* to the *Soul*: And as on high,
> Those rowling Fires *discover* but the Sky
> Not light us *here;* so *Reason's* glimmering Ray
> Was lent, not to *assure* our *doubtfull* way,
> But *guide* us upward to a *better Day.*
> And as those nightly Tapers disappear
> When Day's bright Lord ascends our Hemisphere;
> So pale grows *Reason* at *Religions* sight;
> So *dyes,* and so *dissolves* in *Supernatural Light.*
>
> (vv. 1–11)

One reason that this sounds so romantic is that it taught the romantics some vocabulary and some cadences, for instance the "weary, wayworn wanderer" of Poe's *To Helen.* There is also Keats. If "fade away into the forest dim" does not come directly from verses 11 and 1 (which seems to me likely if unprovable: the "Dim" of verse 1 of Dryden's poem stands out memorably, and to fade away is to grow pale and to dissolve), it moves in the spirit of these cadences.[11]

Liquid quantity and liquid slowness hold and move through the first several verses, the gradual turns within the varying pauses increasing and directing the slowness. The power of the imagery works within the meters. The crucial accents touch the crucial words at their exact times. Verses 7 and 11 resolve by returning from the varied pausing to unbroken patterns near the metrical base. The moment of dawn issuing (twice) into full day is a metrical as a religious triumph, and in the best sense a polemical triumph.

One cannot reduce the power of such passages to versification, any more than one can reduce them to doctrine or personal feeling or imagery. Experience is more than the sum of its analyses, and poetry is experienced. The question is, how does so much personal feeling illumine the doctrine in the poems? We can say, through sincerity; we can say, through genius. We cannot perfectly say; if we could, great poetry could be written by mathematicians or structural linguists; but surely an important part of the answer lies in the restless, disclosing, varied seeking for balance, in the surge and resolution of the supremely governed sound.[12]

The greatest test of the heroic couplet is narrative. The forward motion that is the essence of narrative seems to contradict the sharp and discrete definition of the couplet. But, where verse paragraphing is possible, the contradiction is not a necessary one. The passages I have discussed from *The Hind and the Panther* and *Religio Laici* are great narrative, the narrative of autobiography and allegory (for night to change into day is for something to happen), and there is in both of them a sense of forward motion working through a variety of changes.

All poetry is in a way narrative: its own narrative. Poetry moves forward in time. To catch the shape of action within it, it needs to move forward, to be able to slow down, to speed up, to show varied relatings, and to exist in differing divisions (paragraphs). The heroic couplet can do all of these. It is particularly suited to reflect the variety of motion, as each motion is felt within and against the norm. The tendency to do things in twos, a real though not exclusive capacity of the couplet, fits some action well; for instance, combat is a twoness.

Dryden handles such action with skill; he sometimes plays with the meanings and names of the actions as in this passage from *Meleager and Atalanta*.

> Two Spears from *Meleager's* Hand were sent,
> With equal Force, but various in th' Event:
> The first was fix'd in Earth, the second stood
> On the Boars bristled Back, and deeply drank his
> Blood.
> Now while the tortur'd Salvage turns around,
> And flings about his Foam, impatient of the Wound,
> The Wounds great Author close at Hand, provokes
> His Rage, and plyes him with redoubled Strokes;
> Wheels as he wheels; and with his pointed Dart
> Explores the nearest Passage to his Heart.
>
> (vv. 192–201)

In verse 193, the two parts of the verse, like the two spears, fare unequally: two normal and firm iambs, against the light writhing of the three feet of "but various in th' Event." [13] The first, "fix'd" spear in verse 194 gets a half-line; the second, striking spear gets a half-line plus the hexameter of verse 195 in which the heaped accents are almost gay in their grisliness. The shifting of movement, dependent on quantity and speed and pausing, winds in and out of the action, getting special prominence in the enjambment, unusually strong for Dryden, of "provokes / His Rage." Boar and man encircle, half-circle, meet head-on. The wheeling wheels, two to two, and the killing is a resolving back to the steady progress of the basically shaped verse 201. This is, of course, a performance,[14] and Dryden expects us to enjoy it as just that; but it also shows the ability of the couplet to do action, be it stoutly performed or fully serious.

The heroic couplet (it is both advantage and defect) tends to accompany action with meditation on action, to interwork the dynamic and static that join in all human action. In general, the strong norms of the couplet and the wide freedom that the couplet allows make it peculiarly fit to render action that involves meditation and the pointing of motive, as when Dryden describes the fight in the woods between Palamon and Arcite in Book II of *Palamon and Arcite* (his version of Chaucer's *Knight's Tale*). I mark the main phrase-end (or phrase-ends, when roughly equal) in each line.

> Now, || at the Time, || and in th' appointed Place,
> The Challenger, and Challeng'd, || Face to Face,
> Approach; || each other from afar they knew,
> And from afar || their Hatred chang'd their Hue.   180
> So stands the *Thracian* Heardsman || with his Spear,
> Full in the Gap, || and hopes the hunted Bear,
> And hears him rustling in the Wood, || and sees
> His Course at Distance || by the bending Trees;
> And thinks, || Here comes my mortal Enemy,   185

And either he must fall in Fight, ||or I:
This while he thinks, || he lifts aloft his Dart;
A gen'rous Chilness || seizes ev'ry Part;
The Veins pour back the Blood, || and fortifie the
    Heart.
Thus pale they meet; || their Eyes with Fury burn; 190
None greets; || for none the Greeting will return:
But in dumb Surliness, || each arm'd with Care
His Foe profest, || as Brother of the War:
Then both, || no Moment lost, || at once advance
Against each other, || arm'd with Sword and
    Lance: 195
They lash, || they foin, || they pass, || they strive to
    bore
Their Corslets, || and the thinnest Parts explore.
Thus two long Hours || in equal Arms || they stood,
And wounded, || wound; || till both were bath'd in
    Blood;
And not a Foot of Ground || had either got,   200
As if the World depended || on the Spot.

The medial phrase-end is, as a norm, abandoned here.
The variety of the placing of phrase-ends is unusual. A
phrase-end occurs after the first syllable once; after the
second syllable five times; after the third, twice; after
the fourth, nine times; after the fifth, only three times;
after the sixth, five times; after the seventh and eighth,
three times each. No phrase-end occurs after the ninth
syllable.

The fundamental norm, the iambic base, is clearly
present. Only verses 183 and 196 are not end-stopped.
Here, as elsewhere in Dryden, the exceptions to end-stopping are so rare that they really cease to be exceptions.
The ear, accustomed to end-stopping and supported by

strong rhymes, supplies at least the shadow of a pause before moving on.

The norm of the medial pause being ignored, the couplet here finds out new and special ways of manifesting balance and emphasis, most impressively in the last six verses.

> They lash, they foin, they pass, they strive to bore
> Their Corslets, and the thinnest Parts explore.
> Thus two long Hours in equal Arms they stood,
> And wounded, wound; till both were bath'd in Blood;
> And not a Foot of Ground had either got,
> As if the World depended on the Spot.
>
> (vv. 196–201)

The first three feet of verse 196, forceful and almost identical to one another in rhythmic value, describe both the vigor of the assault and the immovable determination of the assailants. The remaining verse and a half of the couplet, with enjambment and tortuous accentuation, differs in rhythm and leads from the furious equality of the fight to the hope of each knight to turn the balance in his favor. How far the metrical shift supports the shift in meaning is hard to say, but, plainly, the repetitive power and the variety of the sound in the couplet helps convey the regulated fury of the battle.

In verse 198 "Thus two long Hours" has the greatest quantity, "they stood" the greatest accent, of the three divisions of the verse: the result is an approach to balance in the strong, unbalanced verse. In line 199 "wounded" and "wound" are joined in emphasis by their heavy accent and quantity and their near identity. *Wound* and *ground* are, in Dryden's pronunciation, a true internal rhyme. The emphasis and the unusual phrasing of the first four syllables need some compensation in the rest of the verse; those three feet are forceful with equal accents, the alliteration working as a strong binder: "till *both* were *bath*'d in *B*lood." Verses 200 and 201 are each unbalanced, yet the first three feet of verse 201 repeat with greater force the metrical pattern of the first three feet of verse 200, the sixth syllable being the key accent in each verse. Again, balance is achieved amidst imbalance.

George Williamson finds that Dryden uses medial pause and balanced accent in meditative verse and gains greater freedom in narrative.[15] The fight scene in *Palamon and Arcite* certainly shows such freedom. Williamson's point is useful, but it should not (as Williamson himself says) be pressed. Even in that passage of "free" narrative, we saw Dryden finding diverse kinds of balance within his freedom; and he sometimes renders very violent action in lines that adhere closely to the secondary norm of medial pause and balanced accent, as in this scene from his translation of the *Aeneid*, Book II. Aeneas is retelling the battle within the walls of Troy.

> Through this [a secret passage] we pass, and mount
>   the Tow'r, from whence   625
> With unavailing Arms the *Trojans* make defence.
> From this the trembling King had oft descry'd
> The *Grecian* Camp, and saw their Navy ride.
> Beams from its lofty height with Swords we hew;
> Then wrenching with our hands, th' Assault re-
>   new.   630
> And where the Rafters on the Columns meet,
> We push them headlong with our Arms and Feet:
> The Lightning flies not swifter than the Fall;
> Nor Thunder louder than the ruin'd Wall:

Down goes the top at once; the *Greeks* beneath   635
Are piecemeal torn, or pounded into Death.
Yet more succeed, and more to death are sent;
We cease not from above, nor they below relent.

Of the fourteen verses, two (verses 626 and 638) are
hexameters with the normal caesura after the sixth syllable; three (verses 631, 632, and 634) have a phrase-end
after the fifth syllable with two heavy accents on either
side; two couplets (verses 627–28 and 635–36) have the
pause after the sixth syllable in the first verse balanced
by a pause after the fourth syllable in the second verse.
Only one couplet (verses 629–30) distinctively departs
from the norm of medial pause and balanced verse. Yet
these verses, for all their tendency to symmetry, convey
swift and varied action. The writing is everywhere competent; one couplet, which, with almost arithmetic neatness, combines the primary base in the first line with the
secondary norm in the second, is superbly resonant poetry, one of Dryden's many successful and perceptive
handlings of the imagery of physical nature.

| The Light | ning flies | not swif | ter than | the Fall; |
                         i i i *i* i

| Nor Thun | der lou | der || than | the ru | in'd Wall: |
                         i i *i* i i

(vv. 633–34)

Dryden also has his failures. His failures of haste and
of conception, of imagery and of diction are frequent
and have often been remarked. Metrical failures are
rare; only a very few of them spring from the peculiar
temptations or limitations of the heroic couplet.

The ability of the couplet to force two elements of meaning into equal prominence can lead the sense to a parallelism or antithesis that is unreal or facile and may falsify nature. Cortez says, in Dryden's *The Indian Emperor*, speaking of Mexico (emphasis mine):

> Here nature spreads her fruitful sweetness round,
> *Breathes* on the air, and *broods* upon the ground.[16]

The distinction, if pretty, is illusory. Later in the play Cortez says (emphasis mine):

> Even lust and envy sleep; yet love denies
> *Rest* to my soul, and *slumber* to my eyes.[17]

One would be hard pressed to find anything so neatly empty in Dryden's later work. But the heroic couplet can always become dull, if hastily or insensitively handled, especially if the lines and epithets balance too easily, as in some transitional passages of his *Aeneid*. Dryden was apparently in haste to leave behind in Sicily the cowards, women, and old men in the Fifth Book, and succumbs to jingling monotony and a curled and powdered nature whose elegance is no excuse.

> A Priest is added, annual Gifts bestow'd;
> And Groves are planted round his blest Abode.
> Nine days they pass in Feasts, their Temples crown'd;
> And fumes of Incense in the Fanes abound.
> Then, from the South arose a gentle Breeze
> That curl'd the smoothness of the glassy Seas:
> The rising Winds, a ruffling Gale afford,
> And call the merry Marriners aboard.
>
> (vv. 993–1000)

A good deal has been said since Wordsworth, much of it harsh, about neoclassical diction for treating physical nature:[18] its generality, trochaic epithets, chilling periphrases, and the like. Such faults exist in Dryden; not a little of his diction has worn badly, especially, one is tempted to say, the elegantly handsome diction he liked to show off. More is involved than a shift of taste; for by Dryden's fundamental principles, good poetry should do justice to the reality of its subject. The couplet, to a small degree, tempts to such faults, mainly because it can use more padding than blank verse or than short-lined stanzas. But such faults are not native to it; the couplet can describe nature beautifully; and Dryden has much beautiful natural description to offer. If much of his description is (pleasantly or unpleasantly) elegant, much of it is warm or tender or ripe or strangely dark, especially in the range of his best images.

A worse fault of the heroic couplet, though not exactly a metrical fault, is that the couplet, with its possibilities for firm shaping and ringing closes, can be *too good* an instrument for argument. It can make the worse appear the better reason with a flourish. Dryden reasoned well in verse and out, so his failures here are rare (rarer than Pope's); but they are real. Even the great passages in *The Hind and the Panther* suffer some: the fideistic argument, probably the most unmanageable argument Dryden ever attempted, trips on its logic.

> Can I believe eternal God could lye
> Disguis'd in mortal mold and infancy?
> That the great maker of the world could dye?
> And after that, trust my imperfect sense
> Which calls in question his omnipotence?

Can I my reason to my faith compell,
And shall my sight, and touch, and taste rebell?
(Part I, vv. 80–86)

This is great poetry that touches on great truth. And it rings true. But it also imparts absurdity; it is a bad argument. Dryden is involved in inescapable self-inconsistency: he gives reason full power to deduce corollaries from the presumption that faith is superior to reason, while at the same instant denying reason's power to have any say in such matters at all. Faith and reason are distinct and not distinct; each has its valid claims and its limits; they have many relations. The fideistic argument mangles their relations. Nor can one, to justify the poetry, deny that the truth matters. It evidently mattered very much to Dryden personally: he was a devout Christian; and he was convinced as a great neoclassical critic that the only poetry that can truly please must be an image of truth. Yet, at the same time, such a defect is not exactly a poetic defect; it comes from abusing a prime virtue of the heroic couplet: its capacity to adapt convincingly to argument.

That abuse becomes a virtue when Dryden displays the sophistry of Maximin in *Tyrannic Love,* Satan in *The State of Innocence,* Achitophel in *Absalom and Achitophel.* Their arguments sound splendid; one appreciates dramatically what St. Catharine, Eve, and Absalom had to contend with; but the audience knows throughout where the truth lies.

The difficulties of the heroic couplet spring from the very strength of the form. The closed couplet, with its strong sense of identity, can tend to check narrative flow; the very balance and precision with which the couplet can be handled can lead sense to false balance, to false precision, to false description, or to bad arguments; the firm norms can become monotonous.

None of these failures is necessary. Dryden overcomes them all. The couplet, in his hands, is a supple instrument of great range. It does not work only in a poetry of statement, though it can state better than can any other form. It can think, it can move, it can rise. It ranges from lyric to epic.

In fact, its most serious defect in drama is that it is not a poetry of prose. Dryden, in the *persona* of Neander, is bothered by that problem in *An Essay of Dramatic Poesy*. Crites urges that rhyme (which, of course, is what distinguishes the heroic couplet from blank verse) is absurd in homely speeches, such as an order to a servant. Neander spends his greatest ingenuity attempting an answer, but he does not succeed: it is the only objection that Crites makes which he does not demolish. Blank verse can be mixed with prose; blank verse, in Shakespeare's hands, can do the work-a-day functions of prose. The heroic couplet cannot: it always presumes some heightening of feeling. But, having said that, one has stated virtually the only limitation of the form. Yvor Winters finds it as good an epic instrument as blank verse, assigning to the difference in the men the inferiority of Dryden's translation of the *Aeneid* to *Paradise Lost*.[19] Be that as it may, the heroic couplet is an epic instrument. Dryden describes vigorous physical action better than Milton and reasons more clearly. It is Milton's massive sublimity which is beyond him, though Dryden, in the *Aeneid* and elsewhere, has sublime moments. Some of the greatest of them are in *Absalom and Achitophel*.

6

The Event of Things:
Absalom and Achitophel

'ABSALOM AND ACHITOPHEL' is Dryden's greatest poem, and the one in which his mastery of the heroic couplet most dazzlingly appears. It is a poem of a complex kind and a single theme: providence, God's and his workers' providings being monstrously parodied, and it would appear threatened, by the machinations of Satan and his agents. The structure displays the struggles; the arguments, imagery, and rhythms offer intricate praise and blame. To see the poem truly is to see those interworkings within the poem's elusive but unified genre.

What Dryden tells us (piecemeal) about the genre has a special though not infallible [1] authority. His title tells us that the poem is allegorical. He subtitled it *"A Poem,"* by which he meant a narrative poem dealing with serious action. He had said of *Annus Mirabilis* that it should be called *"historical,* not *epic,"* [2] giving as one of his reasons that epic was too bold a title for a poem little longer than a single Iliad. Since *Annus Mirabilis* is

95

longer than *Absalom and Achitophel* and Dryden calls himself *"the Historian"* [5] of *Absalom and Achitophel*, he evidently considered the poem historical rather than epic. The paradox of miniature epic which several critics use,[4] has some point but remains paradox. Epics are big. Dryden wrote that an epic should be of substantial magnitude and with "all things . . . grave, majestical, and sublime." [5] Dryden speaks of the poem as "Satyre" [6] and may have thought of it as "A Satyre against Sedition" (the subtitle of *The Medal*). A satire, by Dryden's later definition,[7] is addressed against a single vice. Blame implicates praise, and much of the poem is overt panegyric. Dryden, himself using a metaphor (the poem as portrait) some critics have fancied, admits the poem's incompleteness when he writes that the *"Frame of it, was cut out, but for a Picture to the Wast."* [8] Its polemical and occasional nature is plain in all Dryden says of it.

Hence we can say that the poem is an occasional, polemical, historical, satirical, panegyrical, truncated, narrative, allegorical poem. That description is hardly lyrical or concise (Polonius might applaud it), but it is accurate as far as it goes, it has Dryden's authority, and may help us understand what such a unique poem is and should be.

A simpler, complementary description is suggested by a passage in "A Discourse Concerning . . . Satire" where Dryden praises Boileau's *Le Lutrin*: "This, I think, my Lord, to be the most beautiful and most noble kind of satire. Here is the majesty of the heroic, finely mixed with the venom of the other; and raising the delight . . . by the sublimity of the expression." [9] He goes on to speak of the need in such poetry for "the beautiful turns of words and thoughts, which are as requisite in this, as in heroic poetry itself, of which the satire is undoubtedly a species."

From this we might call the poem "noble satire" or "heroic satire," or "epic satire"—attractive synonyms. But "satirical heroic poem" is more accurate, since Dryden gives "heroic poetry" as genus, "satire" as species.

Such a kind should be nobly mixed, beautiful and dignified in the turns of meter and rhetoric, capable of high praise and severe blame, of persuasive reasoning, of one subject and with one action, with lesser parts subordinated to the general intent. That intent is to persuade of political and religious truth by presenting an action, an action that expresses and is permeated by the truth, the truth guiding and issuing in "Th' event of things" (v. 935).

The polemics and poetry support and block each other. Insofar as the poem is rhetorically successful, it is successful as polemics. The persuasion must work through the poetic substancing of the poem. But a good poem presents a complete and unified action; and one of the chief aims of this poem is to prevent action. The developing action was incomplete when Dryden wrote; he wanted to use the persuasive power of the poetry to keep the action frustrated. He wanted rebellion not to happen.[10] The poem stands across itself; it almost had to. Nonetheless I feel the frustration as a flaw of the structure of the poem,[11] though, as I shall show, Dryden covers the frustration by working out a lesser paradigmatic action.

The opening section (vv. 1–42) provides a view of David as anointed king, tells us of and polemically "justifies" his promiscuity, and in the brilliant bargain (1)

97

explains the beauty and royal dignity of Absalom and (2) makes clear that he and his claims to the throne are illegitimate. In description fed by narrative, Absalom's marriage and his wild youth are presented. The action has been introduced.

A formal moral sentence touching major themes introduces the complications:

> But Life can never be sincerely blest:
> Heaven punishes the bad, and proves the best.
>
> (vv. 43–44)

The account of the Jewish people follows: it is both a magnificently denigrating "character" and a retrospective narrative of the events which lead up to the Popish plot, which another moral-providential sentence introduces:

> But, when to Sin our byast Nature leans,
> The carefull Devil is still at hand with means;
> And providently Pimps for ill desires:
>
> (vv. 79–81)

The next section narrates in general language the progress of the plot and leads up to the character of Achitophel. His character is followed by an explanation and judgment of his motives and schemes, and by a reminder that the Jews are fickle enough to succumb. All so far, in action and in meaning, leads up to the great temptation scene, where argument becomes high and epic action. The first temptation speech includes much summary of narrative, and predictive narrative. Absalom undergoes his inner moral battle; he declares his loyalty to the king, but slips, in the midst of his speech, back into temptation, and by the end of his own speech has been staggered by his great ambition.

Achitophel presses his advantage and pours in fresh arguments in a long speech divided between predictive narrative, narrative of past events, arguments, and plans. Absalom is convinced. The framework of the conversion of Absalom, which is the true and great action realized in the poem, is biblical, Edenic, Miltonic,[12] and also in driving, half-hidden metaphors, military. Though the action is "only" argument, it has Aristotelian completeness in the felt weight of the great political and religious issues involved, and in the conflict, building, turn, and release. Everything through verse 490 has built, in active and dialectical rhythms, toward an action (which is not to occur).

Then comes the change. The plot is to become "a Pageant Show" (v. 751), a "War in Masquerade" (v. 752).[13] So does the poem. "To farther this" (v. 491) Achitophel "Unites / The Malecontents" (vv. 491–92), brilliantly characterized by Dryden first as classes (vv. 495–542)—noble but mistaken, foolish, vicious, hot-headed and thoughtless followers and tools—then as individuals (vv. 544–681). Characters, motives, and moral understanding are offered. "Surrounded thus . . . / Deluded *Absalom*, forsakes the Court" (vv. 682–83), and the progress, the war in masquerade begins, a progress not of epic war, but as verse 444 has foreshadowed, a "Progress in the Peoples Hearts." The people, awed and likewise deluded, are "dazled" (v. 686). In a couplet which echoes and sums the poem so far, and repeats the language of verse 444, "Thus, form'd by Nature [as in the poem's opening and the character of Absalom], furnish'd out with Arts [supplied with industrious deviltry by Achitophel], / He [Absalom] glides unfelt into their secret hearts" (vv. 692–93). This progress produces a speech, which by the "Youth, Beauty, Graceful Action" of Absalom (v. 723), but more tellingly by "Common Interest" (v. 724), prevails. Absalom makes a Progress as a (false) Messiah, prophesied by Achitophel, a false prophet, in the temptation scene. Evil charmingly and blasphemously is prevailing. "Thus, in a Pageant Show, a Plot is made; / And Peace it self is War in Masquerade" (vv. 751–52).

What can prevent the triumph of that "war"? Nothing save a counterprogress, a turning to reason, to true supporters, to the one who rules by genuine right. The rest of the poem is, precisely, that counterprogress, and in a way unlike that of any other poem I know, its own action. The action, the counteraction, *is* the persuasion Dryden variously offers.

The mounting danger causes the narrator to break his calm survey, to speak in the name of reason and justice, to cry out prophetically "Oh foolish *Israel!*" (v. 753), then to offer a powerful defense, in his proper person, of the truth (vv. 753–810).

The danger yet looms, so much so that the next transition is begun by a near desperate question and exclamation: "Now what Relief can Righteous *David* bring? / How Fatall 'tis to be too good a King!" (vv. 811–12). His supporters, if noble, are few; and Barzillai's son is dead. That death appears to mean logically certain defeat, since "War was all . . . [his] Own" (v. 841). The relation of Barzillai's son to Barzillai bears a striking ana-

100

logue in reverse (especially in vv. 829–31) to that of Absalom to his father; Barzillai's son is described in language reminiscent of Milton's angels, "Oh Ancient Honour, Oh Unconquer'd Hand" (v. 844).[14] His death and triumphal ascent to heaven are the metaphysical turning point of the poem, bringing celestial support (vv. 852–53).

Though the promise is there, the human situation remains fearful. The small faithful band (vv. 864–916) dares resist the "powerful Engines bent, / To batter down the lawful Government" (vv. 917–18). The stage is set, after a terse summary (vv. 919–32), for David, "revolving, in his carefull Breast, / Th' event of things" (vv. 934–35), at last, awfully, to speak. His speech, which is the height of the counterprogress, wins (prophetically and under God's consent) the people's hearts. All shall be well.

The pageant show is too much pageant, and I find the narrative-epic rhythms more powerful to verse 490 than afterwards. The flight to heaven, crucial to the resolution of the poem, is a flight that fails, especially in the mimetic hexameter of verse 851. Nor is the poem's timing flawless. The end—however well prepared for in argument and in the convening of action and thought— still comes too abruptly. As Johnson saw, the drama is solved by too rapidly magic a magic. Yet the masquerade war is a brilliant solution to an all but insoluble problem: the action must be blocked, yet occur. Further, our dissatisfaction may come in some true part from our failure, not Dryden's, to respond to the majesty of noble argument. The argument leads to a complete action, an action that is thought, persuasion, right, divine authority. As Bernard Schilling tells us, what needs to be said has been said.[15]

The poem cannot be judged only as a heroic action, for, as we have seen, it is a mixed kind of poem. It includes satire, and satire is a baggy hunting sack, which has one principle, instructive blame, but no inherent shape. Dryden was informed and shrewd in the traditions of satire, and the poem offers examples of all or almost all the traditional features defined in the following passage by Mary Claire Randolph. The inserted verse references show one example of each feature.

> To illustrate his thesis, win his case, and move his audience . . . , the Satirist utilizes miniature dramas [vv. 1006–1009], sententious proverbs and quotable maxims [vv. 809–10], compressed beast fables [vv. 445–54] . . . , brief sermons [vv. 192–99], sharp debates [vv. 315–72], . . . "characters" [vv. 583–629], . . . little fictions and apologues [vv. 953–56], visions [vv. 850–63], apostrophes [vv. 632–35] and invocations to abstractions [vv. 844–45].[16]

Several of these devices also appear, Satanically turned and tuned, within the speeches of Achitophel; and parodies of several of them appear in Achitophel's arguments and in such passages as the wondrous mockvision of the visionary Corah:

> But, where the witness faild, the Prophet Spoke:
> Some things like Visionary flights appear;
> The Spirit caught him up, the Lord knows where:
> (vv. 655–57)

In short, here is God's—and the devil's—plenty of rhetorical devices, all having the polemical unity of expressing complex praise and more complex blame in favor of the true and royal cause and against Shaftesburian and Whigamore machinations, cruelties, and lunacies. I doubt that there would be much complaint about the order of the poem, if the poem were merely satire, since it has a gorgeous sufficiency of satiric devices and the thematic unity a satire requires (satire as such not requiring a unity of progress), were it not for the magnificent arc of the incompleted heroic action.

The bedrock method of satire and panegyric, underlying all the range and clustering of brilliant technique, is simply statement and argument. How do we know that Jonas is wicked and Shimei more so? Because the poem says so: "But he [Jonas], tho bad, is follow'd by a worse [Shimei]" (v. 583). How are we to learn that the King is right? The narrator and the King argue that he is.

Argument unifies by theme, by pointing the topic, by being for or against something. Within itself, an argument does not proceed purely by strict entailment. The arrangement of topics may be fairly loose in logical sequence, but a persuasive argument should sound highly coherent and reasonable. Achieving this, as Dryden normally does, is a matter of logic and evidence, of thematic unity, of rhetoric, meter, and tone, and of other sorts of linkings and successions. The opening of Absalom's speech is a relatively simple example.

> He thus reply'd—And what Pretence have I
> To take up Arms for Publick Liberty?
> My Father Governs with unquestion'd Right;
> The Faiths Defender, and Mankinds Delight:
> Good, Gracious, Just, observant of the Laws;
> And Heav'n by Wonders has Espous'd his Cause.

103

Whom has he Wrong'd in all his Peaceful Reign?
Who sues for Justice to his Throne in Vain?
What Millions has he Pardon'd of his Foes,
Whom Just Revenge did to his Wrath expose?
Mild, Easy, Humble, Studious of our Good;
Enclin'd to Mercy, and averse from Blood.

(vv. 315–26)

The thesis is stated so plainly in verse 317 that nothing remains of the case for rebellion except Shaftesbury's malignant and irrational cleverness. It is absurd to question an unquestioned right. For Dryden to call "unquestioned" the right being questioned is the obverse absurdity, but then Dryden is tossing, if not palming, the coin. The divine and human intermix and support in what follows, the evidence for the thesis. Charles-David is "The Faiths Defender" and "Mankinds Delight." He is "Good, Gracious, Just" (God's vicegerent in goodness and justice and gracious through God's grace), "observant of the Laws" (the laws human and divine, the human laws deriving their authority from the divine, and benefiting human beings). The "Wonders," providential signs of favor such as those celebrated in *Annus Mirabilis*, are powerful evidence, in the context of assumption accepted by all parties to the debate, for the truth of the thesis, and support the view that the sovereign, being legitimate, rules under God's Providence and with God's sanction. The next four lines (vv. 321–24) are rhetorical questions (tightly balanced in meter and the rhetoric, each beginning with a similar pronoun) giving evidence that the king possesses the list of qualities of the subsequent verses (325–26). The argument in this passage is basically simple: David should rule, because (1) he is the legitimate ruler; (2) he fits the qualities of an ideal king (the qualities of such a king are listed, and evidence given for them); (3) providence has witnessed in his favor; (4) his foes are wicked and deserve his wrath. The points shrewdly interlace. For instance, the assertion that David's enemies still deserve his wrath (have not yet been punished) is evidence that David has one of the requisite moral qualities: mercy.

The metrical and rhetorical connections strengthen the sense of logical stoutness. Metrical placing and repeated sounds put items together. "Pretence" taints "Publick Liberty," "Father" and "Faiths" go together, as do "Defender" and "Delight." "Good, Gracious, Just," "Mild, Easy, Humble," are lists which fit the man and each other. The contrast between "Mercy" and "Blood" is plain and severe (it hides a not overly merciful threat). His quality "Good" beginning verse 319 becomes the people's "Good," ending verse 325. The rhetorical questions and similarly placed pronouns help frame the motion of a passage which puts "Mercy" and "Good" against "Wrong" and "Blood." The substantial feel of the argument including the grammatical subordering persuades the reader that the thesis is true and that overwhelming and judicious evidence has been offered (though, in fact, no particular item of evidence has arrived).

The very sense of poetic coherence can be persuasive, as when Achitophel says, "Believe me, Royal Youth, thy Fruit must be, / Or gather'd Ripe, or rot upon the Tree" (vv. 250–51). The metrical force of locked and alliterative parallels, and the logical shape of the disjunction make it difficult to refuse the choice in the terms, including the metaphor, which the wily tempter offers.

Dryden would make us simultaneously feel the persua-

sive power of the argument, to feel some but not too
much sympathy for the partly innocent victim,[17] and yet
feel within the whole context that Shaftesbury's arguments are sophistry, that Shaftesbury is using "studied
Arts" (v. 228). Dryden would have us aware of such
arts, aware enough to see through Achitophel-Shaftes-
bury, but not aware enough to see through Dryden's own
arts, even when Dryden comes very near dishonesty (as
in "To Compass this the Triple Bond he broke; . . . .
And fitted *Israel* for a Foreign Yoke" (vv. 175, 177),[18] or
when, more slyly, he convinces us that Achitophel is
wrong in argument, without either presenting or answer-
ing the arguments.

> By buzzing Emissaries, fills the ears
> Of listning Crowds, with Jealosies and Fears
> Of Arbitrary Counsels brought to light,
> And proves the king himself a *Jebusite:*
> Weak Arguments! which yet he knew full well,
> Were strong with People easie to Rebell.
> For, govern'd by the *Moon,* the giddy *Jews*
> Tread the same track when she the Prime renews:
> And once in twenty Years, their Scribes Record,
> By natural Instinct they change their Lord.
>   (vv. 210–19)

The King was possibly at that time a "Jebusite" in persuasion or tendency. He may have pledged at the secret
Treaty of Dover to become a Roman Catholic; and he
died one.[19] More to the rhetorical issue, Achitophel
buzzes into ears like the biblical and Miltonic serpent
that he is, but we do not hear his arguments nor Dryden's answer. The scorn of "Weak Arguments!" and the

denouncing contempt for the fickleness of the English covers the unlogic of the persuading. If Dryden knew any arguments that the King was a Roman Catholic or was encouraging that cause, he was well advised not to advertise them.[20]

The arguments are inwardly strong of rhetorical ordering. They move in dramatic conflict against each other, especially in the temptation scene. They contribute to the texture of structure; throughout the poem the same issues and reasons are worked and rewoven. They reveal character; they justify the satire and panegyric; they provide the clearest statements of themes and convictions which underlie and penetrate the formal designs, small and large, created in imagery, meter, and rhetoric.

Imagery is functional; it is subordinate. It bears and empowers theme and meaning; it is in the best sense ornament to the argument; in its repetitions and variety it is and enters rhythm. As biblical allegory, the poem exists within a large comparison; [21] it is woven by laden, reminding images.

The basic function of the imagery is praise and blame of the good and evil parties: the basic image is the allegory itself, in which one party is seen under the providence of God, the other under the providing of the devil. The allegory is historical; it is comparison; it is universal. The same political truths and providence are, Dryden finds, at work in London as in Jerusalem. The allegory becomes identity. Dryden is talking about an actual political situation; the Earl of Shaftesbury would have been more than moderately surprised to have discovered that neither he nor Achitophel, but some mysterious third gentleman, was under fire.²² Yet at the same time the poem transcends its situation and its targets; its realm of existence is not merely political and local, but poetic and permanent.

The imagery supports the contrast drawn between David and Achitophel. David rules by the authority of nature and law, in accordance with reason, in his proper place, under God. Achitophel, like rebellion generally, is "unfixt in Principles and Place" (v. 154), without authority, irrationally motivated, out of place and seeking the overthrow of true hierarchy, under the devil.

The king is the truest image of deity, as king (v. 792) and as man (vv. 10, 32). Achitophel is one of those like "Feinds . . . harden'd in Impenitence" (v. 145); he images Lucifer. The apple of Eden which Lucifer tempts the people and Absalom to take appears at least twice (vv. 200–203, 250–51). The sun suggests kingship in the stable order of nature (vv. 686, 728–35); the moon suggests lunacy, melancholy, rebellion, caprice, the attempted overthrow of order (vv. 216–19, 787–90).

The moon likewise suggests tides, a meaningless and capricious determinism. Just after the Jews have been condemned because they are "govern'd by the *Moon*" (v. 216) and consequently change their lord every twenty years, Whiggism is seen as an ebbtide (and hence under the moon's dominion). The Whigs would keep the king dependent on the crowd so "That Kingly power, thus ebbing out, might be / Drawn to the dregs of a Democracy" (vv. 226–27).

Moon, tide, and ugly behavior recur in another image.

> What Standard is there in a fickle rout,
> Which, flowing to the mark, runs faster out?

Not only Crowds, but Sanhedrins may be
Infected with this publick Lunacy:
And Share the madness of Rebellious times,
To Murther Monarchs for Imagin'd crimes.

(vv. 785–90)

Verrall shows that this image refers to the tide's reaching its high-water mark and receding (the "Lunacy" suggesting again the moon's influence).[23] "Rout," one may add in support of Verrall, can mean both an unruly crowd and the sea's roaring. But neither this nor the preceding image stays simple: in the previous image, the dregs suggest casks or boiling tubs rather than the sea (touching on the traditional imagery for melancholy and enthusiasm);[24] in this image, the secondary metaphor of "Infected" is to illness (again referring to melancholy, like verse 926), and in the tide metaphor there is at least a hint of boiling over (melancholy once more). The struggle of the sea against its bounds is itself among the oldest Christian and classical metaphors for the conflict between the chaos of disordered passion and the rule of moral law.

Some of these tangling suggestions occur in one of the best comparisons of the poem.

This Plot, which fail'd for want of common Sense,
Had yet a deep and dangerous Consequence:
For, as when raging Fevers boyl the Blood,
The standing Lake soon floats into a Flood;
And every hostile Humour, which before
Slept quiet in its Channels, bubbles o'r:
So, several Factions from this first Ferment,
Work up to Foam, and threat the Government.

(vv. 134–41)

The beast imagery aimed at the rebels, though more sparing than that in *The Medal*[25] and *The Hind and the Panther*, is fierce enough. Verrall has pointed out the contempt for the people, envisaged as insects,[26] in one of the speeches in which Achitophel tempts Absalom:

> Behold him [David] setting in his Western Skies,
> The Shadows lengthning as the Vapours rise.
> He is not now, as when on *Jordan*'s Sand
> The Joyfull People throng'd to see him Land,
> Cov'ring the *Beach*, and blackning all the *Strand:*
> But, like the Prince of Angels from his height,
> Comes tumbling downward with diminish'd light.
>
> (vv. 268–74)

Achitophel, attempting to darken the glory of the regal sun, succeeds in blackening the people and himself. The last image names his supporter in that dark attempt.

The Levites are the leaders of the pack, "tho not of surest scent, / Yet deepest mouth'd against the Government" (vv. 527–28). A scorn as great and a more belittling contempt is directed at the tools, "the herd of such, / Who think too little, and who talk too much" (vv. 533–34). And Corah, worst villain of all, is likened to Moses' serpent (and hence by curious implication to that old Serpent the devil) in a magnificent, terrible, and —for once!—accurate prophecy. "Erect thy self" is, I suspect, the most savage and the most proper sexual pun Dryden ever made.

> Yet, *Corah,* thou shalt from Oblivion pass;
> Erect thy self thou Monumental Brass:
> High as the Serpent of thy mettall made,
> While Nations stand secure beneath thy shade.
>
> (vv. 632–35)

Fertility and barrenness suggest good and evil, but not simply. The barrenness of Michal, "A Soyl ungratefull to the Tiller's care" (v. 12), provides an excuse for David's promiscuity and perversely connotes some blame for Queen Catherine ("ungrateful"). Barrenness becomes more deeply evil in David's speech in an image that Verrall praises.[27]

> But save me most from my Petitioners.
> Unsatiate as the barren Womb or Grave;
> God cannot Grant so much as they can Crave.
> (vv. 986–88)

Nymphomania allied with death is a hungry evil.

At least twice the biblical parable of the sower enters an image. In the lament for Achitophel's fall from his excellence as a judge, occur these lines.

> Oh, had he been content to serve the Crown,
> With vertues only proper to the Gown;
> Or, had the rankness of the Soyl been freed
> From Cockle, that opprest the Noble seed:
> (vv. 192–95)

These lines emphasize Achitophel's demonic ill will by showing how far he fell. A more involved, but similar, image is used to give some justification to Absalom:

> Desire of Power, on Earth a Vitious Weed,
> Yet, sprung from High, is of Caelestial Seed:
> (vv. 305–306)

One witnesses here a fundamental belief of the poem, that evil is a perversion of good, a belief even more vividly caught in a range of images of gold. Gold is a

good, metaphorical, natural, and economic; a good
which greed and idolatry are rabid to pervert.

> [The Jews] wondred why, so long, they had obey'd
> An Idoll Monarch which their hands had made:
> Thought they might ruine him they could create;
> Or melt him to that Golden Calf, a State.
>
> (vv. 63–66)

> In his [any god's] defence his Servants [priests] are
>   as bold
> As if he had been born of beaten gold.
>
> (vv. 102–103)

> *Achitophel*, grown weary to possess
> A lawfull Fame, and lazy Happiness;
> Disdain'd the Golden fruit to gather free,
> And lent the Croud his Arm to shake the Tree.
>
> (vv. 200–203)

> Th' Ambitious Youth, too Covetous of Fame,
> Too full of Angells Metal in his Frame
>
> (vv. 309–10)

> His Right, for Sums of necessary Gold,
> Shall first be Pawn'd, and afterwards be Sold:
>
> (vv. 405–406)

> His Hand [Shimei's] a Vare of Justice did uphold;
> His Neck was loaded with a Chain of Gold.
>
> (vv. 595–96)

> [David], brib'd with petty summs of Forreign Gold,
> Is grown in *Bathsheba*'s Embraces old:
>
> (vv. 709–10)

(The last quotation, though put in Monmouth's mouth,
had enough truth in it to suggest some boldness in Dry-

den and some callousness in Charles.) These images almost make a poem of their own, and focus one of the
poem's deepest themes: evil perverts good. That metaphysical conviction is a major ground of the action, of
the judgment of the action, of the allegorical imagery,
and of much of the particular imagery. Even those images, such as melancholy and boiling, which are not
especially biblical, serve biblical-historical ways of
seeing. Providence is central in the poem.

The devil's providence of blasphemy and evil, often
with sexual hints (though sex is not primary in Dryden's
view of evil), is a major theme of the poem, overtly
stated.

> But, when to Sin our byast Nature leans,
> The carefull Devil is still at hand with means;
> And providently Pimps for ill desires.
>
> (vv. 79–81)

The rebels are shown as blasphemous and evil in some
astonishing verses, and Dryden shades into blasphemies
and sophistries of his own.

The opening passage is fantastically clever (even to
the realm of romantic fantasy) and deliberately sophisti-
cal, wittily and disingenuously handling the tricky set of
problems and advantages created by Charles's promiscuity and Monmouth's illegitimacy. David lived in a time
"When Nature prompted, and no law deny'd / Promis-
cuous use of Concubine and Bride" (vv. 5–6). Dryden
knew, unmistakably, that he was engaged in sophistry.
For several times in other works he shows up a villain
for sophistically identifying "natural" (according to im-
pulse) and "natural" (according to moral law). Maximin,

113

Nourmahal, Don Sebastian (who admits the sophistry a moment after he utters it), and Myrrha, all employ the dodge in order to justify their wickedness.[28]

The same sophistry, given a twist, shortly after fits Monmouth.

> What e'r he did was done with so much ease,
> In him alone, 'twas Natural to please.
> His motions all accompanied with grace;
> And *Paradise* was open'd in his face.
> With secret Joy, indulgent *David* view'd
> His Youthfull Image in his Son renew'd:
>
> (vv. 27–32)

The suggestion is that the natural (illegitimate) son must have more "natural" graces and excellences than a legal heir. A further suggestion of the "Natural" is a commonplace. So Dryden praises the "artless" art of Lee[29] and Oldham[30] and Otway.[31] Here he touches more than commonplace feeling, praising Absalom in two of Dryden's favorite images, which are also central images of the poem: paradise and kingship, in both of which nature and politics are submitted to the holy ordering of Providence. It is a lovely passage, but it enters blasphemy, possibly in the strange working of "Natural" and "*Paradise*," and surely in the likening in the last couplet of David-Absalom to God-Christ. To be sure, David, by Dryden's sincere political conviction, was God's vicegerent; but Charles's office as vicegerent is one thing, Charles as "natural" father something else again.

Achitophel uses the same sort of blasphemy (seen by Dryden and the reader as blasphemy) when he offers Messiahship to Absalom. The climactic verse 240 ("Thee, *Saviour*, Thee, the Nations Vows confess") is picked up ironically and gracefully by the narrator later, especially in verses 727–28:

> The Croud, (that still believe their Kings oppress)
> With lifted hands their young *Messiah* bless.

The crowd is positive that kings always ("still") oppress, but with an exalted stupidity hasten to bless the King-they-think-to-come.

The sneer at Catholics in verses 120–21 ("Such savory Deities must needs be good, / As serv'd at once for Worship and for Food") is a variant of a commonplace Protestant sneer of the day,[32] but a plainly blasphemous one, at odds with verse 87 ("And their's the Native right—") and with the attack on Lord Howard for having taken the sacraments blasphemously ("And Canting *Nadab* let Oblivion damn, / Who made new porridge for the Paschal Lamb," vv. 575–76). Polemics has the best of more than one world.

The characters of Shimei and Corah bristle with blasphemies ingrown in their natures. Verses 624–25 and 650–51 are two of the most brilliant.

> For Towns once burnt, such Magistrates require
> As dare not tempt Gods Providence by fire.
>
> His Memory, miraculously great,
> Could Plots, exceeding mans belief, repeat.

What the blasphemy of the rebels means is defined in one of the poem's most important statements.

> If ancient Fabricks nod, and threat to fall,
> To Patch the Flaws, and Buttress up the Wall,
> Thus far 'tis Duty; but here fix the Mark:
> For all beyond it is to touch our Ark.

> To change Foundations, cast the Frame anew,
> Is work for Rebels who base Ends pursue:
> At once Divine and Humane Laws controul;
> And mend the Parts by ruine of the Whole.
> The Tampering World is subject to this Curse,
> To Physick their Disease into a worse.
>
> (vv. 801–10)

The view of politics expressed in these verses is not, despite Bredvold,[33] fearfully prudential, but providential. The "ark" and the "curse" carry the full weight of biblical meaning,[34] strengthened by the allegorical-theological framing and grounding of the poem. Revolution against present order is not to Dryden in itself evil (as Dryden's "The Lady's Song" proves beyond quibble); but revolution against a legitimate order founded on divine sanction and natural law is destructive of the divine and human fabric of political justice. The attack is, precisely, blasphemous, and there Dryden rests his case and founds and centers the poem.

In the poem, as we have seen, blasphemy is not only shown as an evil: it intrudes. The problem involved, a theological, ethical, political, and esthetic problem, is best shown by the most deliberately and flagrantly hideous verses in the poem.

> By their own arts 'tis Righteously decreed,
> Those dire Artificers of Death shall bleed.
> Against themselves their Witnesses will Swear,
> Till Viper-like their Mother Plot they tear:
> And suck for Nutriment that bloody gore
> Which was their Principle of Life before.
> Their *Belial* with their *Belzebub* will fight;
> Thus on my Foes, my Foes shall do me Right:
>
> (vv. 1010–17)

What Dryden defends here is Charles's having people killed by having other people tell lies about them. That is to say, he evilly defends the indefensibly evil. Yet the verses as poetry are stunningly able; they fit structurally, are a climax of evil (creating a genuine shape of action); and they do represent a devilish sort of justice. To die by one's own device is in some sense an example of obvious justice, of what we even call "poetic justice." Those who have innocent people killed by the deliberate use of perjured witnesses are not exactly nice people and do not deserve kind treatment. The Whigs were doing just that. But he who uses such methods enters their world of evil and here Dryden does so with enormous, if unpleasant, poetic power. So does he elsewhere, if not so grimly, in the polemical windings and shadings of the poem. That he does so matters as truth and therefore, finally, as poetic judgment. But how brilliantly he moves!

The verses are metrically complicated. In verse 1010 evil hisses through the arts of righteousness. Verse 1011 is in its harshness and merciless linkings one of the fiercest verses Dryden or anyone else ever made. "Artificers" is a supremely awkward and brisk word, and the forcible ties of *th-sh* and other sounds lead to the plain force and meaning of "bleed."

1 2 3 4   4 5 2 42 5 3 1   6 6 3
Those dire Artificers of Death shall bleed.

Verses 1012–15 imitate their own action, move against themselves, inversions of syntax and shifts of subject acting out the switchings, caught firm in the wonderful, opposed, alike names of *Belial* and *Belzebub* (for this line a better form than "Beelzebub"). The verses are at-

tracted into the oppositions within verse 1017, demon-
strating on our metrical pulses that the word "Right"
which clinches the passage is right, and monstrously
wrong, its own antithesis.

As was earlier said, one can overrate the importance
of balance and antithesis in the metrical workings of the
heroic couplet. But they are important, and Dryden has
some special occasions for them in the poem. He would
persuade us he offers a balanced view between the noise
of extremes; in the Popish Plot itself there is truth and
falsity on either side. Something—we shall probably
never know what or how severe—was likely afoot; [35]
Oates and Bedloe were monstrous liars; Shaftesbury and
company did stir up and cash in on fears occasioned by
the testimony and by Sir Edmund Berry Godfrey's most
foul and unnatural murder (or suicide).[36] Charles was
using the Plot in more than one way, permitting the
prosecutions and condemning the Whigs for inciting
them.[37]

> From hence began that Plot, the Nation's Curse,
> Bad in it self, but represented worse.
> Rais'd in extremes, and in extremes decry'd;
> With Oaths affirm'd, with dying Vows deny'd.
> Not weigh'd, or winnow'd by the Multitude;
> But swallow'd in the Mass, unchew'd and Crude.
> Some Truth there was, but dash'd and brew'd with
>   Lyes;
> To please the Fools, and puzzle all the Wise.
> Succeeding times did equal folly call,
> Believing nothing, or believing all.
>
> (vv. 108–17)

Energy, variety, balance. And "Curse." Oates is accursed,
but the Plot is also the Nation's Curse, God's visitation

of judgment (as punishment or trial—see verse 44). Verse 110 gets to as near a balance as a five-foot line can afford. It is chiastic: "Rais'd" "extremes" "extremes" "cry'd." A B B A. The two stresses on either side of the medial pause are exact of equality in stress, in syntax, in final consonants and in the repeated word, and in political force. Verse 115 is almost as equally balanced, and the shift of pausing and of metrical motion in the verses in between those framing verses is the surge of contrary energies meant. The longer view, posterity's, in the last couplet, quiets down, and soberly balances.

The poem's judgment of the Jews (the English) is metrical and pungent:

> The *Jews*, a Headstrong, Moody, Murmuring race,
> As ever try'd th' extent and stretch of grace;
> God's pamper'd people whom, debauch'd with ease,
> No King could govern, nor no God could please;
> (Gods they had tri'd of every shape and size
> That God-smiths could produce, or Priests devise:)
>
> (vv. 45–50)

The epithets of verse 45 are strong, lingered over; "Murmuring" is onomatopoeic. "Stretch," a surprising extension of the metaphor "extent," requires a new pause and takes the verse beyond the first pause and the ear's normal expectation. The effect is mildly imitative (the phrasing is a bit stretched) and clearly emphatic. "God's pamper'd people" piles up heavy accents that force the mind to attend the mock-epic relations. The alliteration of the *p*'s expresses a special shade of contempt, here and elsewhere in the poem ("providently Pimps," v. 82; "Popularly prosecute the Plot," v. 490, "popularly" being a weakly ugly rumble Dryden delighted at—see also vv. 336, 689). The parallelism of "God" and "King" suggests the analogies on which the poem relies; the prominent negative words stress the negation of true order by rebellion. The inverted foot that places heavy stress on "Gods" in "Gods they had tri'd" underwrites the outlandish play on "Gods." The Jews lack the wit to tell God from the false gods. Verses 49 and 50 fairly hiss with contempt.

As potently harsh are the verses about Corah, which suggest, by metrics as well as by a half-submerged ambiguity of language, that prodigies can be monstrous as well as divine.

> Prodigious Actions may as well be done
> By Weavers issue, as by Princes Son.
> (vv. 638–39)

The harshness of "Prodigious" casts doubt on the excellence of the actions for which Corah is satirically praised; the metrical and grammatical parallelism of "Weavers issue" and "Princes Son" enforces a contrast rather than a likeness: Corah is base in birth and in moral substance.

In the character of Zimri (the Duke of Buckingham), the sprawling and metrically unparallel list of qualities fit the man.

> But, in the course of one revolving Moon,
> Was Chymist, Fidler, States-Man and Buffoon:
> Then all for Women, Painting, Rhiming, Drinking;
> Besides ten thousand freaks that dy'd in thinking.
> (vv. 549–52)

The moon hints his inconstancy. The lists show, very positively, his complete disregard of order, seriousness, hierarchy. The peculiar imbalance of the last items in the two lists strikes the ear: "Buffoon" contrasts with the other words in its list by being an iambic word; "Drinking" keeps the trochaic pattern of its list and brings out the comic possibilities of a feminine ending.

The beginning verses of the most famous character in the poem are as magnificent in versification as in imagery and metaphysical detestation.[38]

> Of these the false *Achitophel* was first:
> A Name to all succeeding Ages Curst.
> For close Designs, and crooked Counsels fit;
> Sagacious, Bold, and Turbulent of wit:
> Restless, unfixt in Principles and Place;
> In Power unpleas'd, impatient of Disgrace.
> A fiery Soul, which working out its way,
> Fretted the Pigmy Body to decay:
> And o'r inform'd the Tenement of Clay.
>
> (vv. 150–58)

Restless and shifting energy rises through the passage to climax and rest in the triplet. The formal introductory couplet gains much of its strength from the high seriousness which sets off the various shades of irony that follow. The devilish and the Miltonic are called to mind by the fact that Achitophel is first of a false crew, and cursed: [39] the rhyme intensifies the suggestion. The "first Curst" was Satan. Varied phrasing and strong accents strengthen lines 152–53 and all that follows. The two inversions in the first foot of lines 154 and 157 are important. "Restless" is perhaps the key word in the passage; strengthened by inversion and the pause that sets it off, it nearly balances with the remaining four feet of the line which define the essence of the rebellious party:

"unfixt in Principles and Place." The metrics reecho the driving emotion of the meaning. Even stronger is "Fretted." In each of the four lines (153–56) preceding it, a pause or phrase-end occurs after the fourth syllable, setting up a mild expectancy which line 157 shatters. The change of pattern and the inversion give a very heavy prominence to "Fretted," an unusual and important word, suggestive of the animallike fierceness of the soul that has eaten through and wasted its own body as it would the structure of the state. The next line is relatively smooth and balanced and, like other closing lines of triplets, provides a rest for the ear. But the line does not attain complete resolution. The metrical balance is imperfect; the diction, idea, and image are very special; and the richly sounded "o'r inform'd" contrasts with the lighter "Tenement," supporting the paradox of a soul that crushes its body beneath its weight.

Verrall has analyzed very skillfully the opening address of Achitophel to Absalom. He shows how lines 230–39 hover around a medial pause, setting a musical pattern which provides contrast with the succeeding lines that depart from the pattern.

> Auspicious Prince! at whose Nativity
> Some Royal Planet rul'd the Southern sky;
> Thy longing Countries Darling and Desire;
> Their cloudy Pillar, and their guardian Fire:
> Their second *Moses*, whose extended Wand
> Divides the Seas, and shews the promis'd Land:
> Whose dawning Day, in every distant age,
> Has exercis'd the Sacred Prophets rage:
> The Peoples Prayer, the glad Deviners Theam,
> The Young-mens Vision, and the Old mens Dream!

> Thee, *Saviour,* Thee, the Nations Vows confess;
> And, never satisfi'd with seeing, bless:
>
> (vv. 230–41)

Line 240 breaks the pattern, so that (we may add to Verrall's remarks) the very strong stress given to *"Saviour"* completes the blasphemous typology of the opening lines, the Old Testament prophecies being fulfilled by the coming of the Messiah. The devil can quote scripture to his purposes, so well here that it realizes the standard that condemns him. Yet, at the same time, Absalom is angel touched by deviltry, not yet beyond redeeming. A lucky historical accident led Dryden to a mixed portrayal of Absalom that improves on, and violates, Dryden's normal idea of how much mixture a heroic character may sustain.

That double view of Absalom, reflecting the doubleness of the poem, appears nowhere more clearly than in these lines:

> What cannot Praise effect in Mighty Minds,
> When Flattery Sooths, and when Ambition Blinds!
> Desire of Power, on Earth a Vitious Weed,
> Yet, sprung from High, is of Caelestial Seed:
> In God 'tis Glory: And when men Aspire,
> 'Tis but a Spark too much of Heavenly Fire.
> Th' Ambitious Youth, too Covetous of Fame,
> Too full of Angells Metal in his Frame;
> Unwarily was led from Vertues ways;
> Made Drunk with Honour, and Debauch'd with Praise.
> Half loath, and half consenting to the Ill,
> (For Loyal Blood within him strugled still)
> He thus reply'd— . . .
>
> (vv. 303–15)

123

The fault is Achitophel's; nonetheless, the taint does infect Absalom. Even "Caelestial Seed," its slight ugliness of sound responding by parallelism to "Vitious Weed," hints that infection. Verses 307–308 are the loveliest, the least infected. In verse 308 the long "heavenly" and the long diphthong of "Fire" contribute to a lovely, lingering effect that may or may not image something of Absalom's hesitating mind. In verse 311, the strongly accented "Unwarily" contrasts with the quieter progress of the rest of the line: temptation is strong, the way to perdition smooth. "Half loath, and half consenting to the Ill" reflects metrically the struggle of Absalom's mind, the strong first two syllables almost, but not quite, counteracting the rest of the verse. The impression of a smooth passage to evil is not quite consistent with the impression of struggle, but that is an inconsistency in the human being who succumbs to temptation. The struggle in Absalom, caught by the versification, is between God and the devil, between supernature and the unnatural, reason and passion, filial piety (natural) and ingratitude (unnatural), between good and evil. It reflects, in little, the struggle of the poem, a great poem in which nature and history are tried by evil.

The poem's surface is alive with a tireless brilliance of language and meter and rhetoric, and that brilliance is a force for unity, as broken light across a body of water helps the eye to go. As satire and as debate the poem is unified: it impresses with its persuasiveness and dignity, even when heels are set in disbelief. And much of what it says is true, locally or permanently valuable. In images and topics and meter and their interrelations it moves toward varied kinds of coherence, kinds which meet at thematic foci. In almost all ways, the poem does satisfy and does cohere. As occasional, as polemic, as historical, as satirical, as providential, it stands.

Its defects as a design of action come from the mixture, from the demands of the occasion and the peculiar historical situation, and from its very success as a design of action. If it did not build so well into and through the temptation, readers would not ask, feel and reach for, a completion that is not fulfilled. The action becomes a noble ghost of an action, a warlike dance of thought. We would have, with many shades and shapes worked into a grand design, the play of mind on the "event of things." The poem might have achieved a greater formal unity and coherence if it were a different, and lesser, sort of a poem. But it is what it is: imperfect, fascinating, brilliant, profound—the best political poem in the language.[40]

7

The Gift of Tongues: Three Poems

THREE OTHER POEMS, *Alexander's Feast*, Dryden's translation of *Veni, Creator Spiritus*, and *A Song for St. Cecilia's Day* show further powers of Dryden's art.

The first is the most astonishingly wrought, but not the most satisfying. As genre, it is an English Pindaric Ode,[1] except not strictly that since written to be set to music. As structure, it is a joyous to semiplayful imitation; a festive narrative about a festivity, a storehouse of ordered and gaily disordered sound about the power of music. Is it a mock-opera or a mock-symphony? A bit of both, and some shades (not too many) higher than either. In it Dryden plays with some of his faults, including public bravura, and some of his less successful sorts of imitative harmony.

Imitative harmony like other elements of good poetry, can fall into self-parody. One tires with Van Doren,[2] of Dryden's rebellowing rocks and sounding shores, though no verse of his ever competed with Cowley's "Nor can

126

the glory contain it self in th' endless space," where the line has a running start toward the infinity it represents.[3]

Dryden at times flirts with the comic possibilities of such parody, as in this attack on the crowd in *The Medal*.

> Almighty Crowd, thou shorten'st all dispute;
> Pow'r is thy Essence; Wit thy Attribute!
> Nor Faith nor Reason make thee at a stay,
> Thou leapst o'r all eternal truths, in thy *Pindarique* way!
>
> (vv. 91–94)

The controlled fury of the pentameters make a deadly contrast with the crowd's brainless preference for unlimited freedom, a freedom stated and conveyed by the galloping fourteener. The verse, like the crowd, breaks out from just bounds. To leap over eternal truth is quite a leap.

Dryden maintains control; his nice sense of the possibilities of imitative harmony both for stirring the mind and feelings and for self-parody sustains the elaborate flirtation of sound and sense in *Alexander's Feast*. A chief secret of the poem is the extraordinary balance maintained between the near parody and the more serious feeling. The self-consciousness and good humor of the poem can be shown by almost any passage,[4] as by the mere proliferation in the poem of measures and kinds of feet. I shall illustrate the typical mastery of tone by two fourteeners in the poem.

The verse from *The Medal*, "Thou leapst o'r all eternal truths, in thy *Pindarique* way!" may be contrasted with a fourteener in the Sixth Book of the *Aeneid* offered as a perfectly serious variation:

What Fun'ral Pomp shall floating *Tiber* see,
When, rising from his Bed, he views the sad
    Solemnity!

(vv. 1208–1209)

Between those two extremes are the considerable fourteeners, about Jove and Alexander respectively, in *Alexander's Feast:*

Sublime on Radiant Spires He rode,
    When He to fair *Olympia* press'd:
    And while He sought her snowy Breast:
    Then, round her slender Waste he curl'd,
    And stamp'd an Image of himself, a Sov'raign of the
    World.

(vv. 29–33)

Sooth'd with the Sound the King grew vain;
    Fought all his Battails o'er again;
    And thrice He routed all his Foes; and thrice He slew
    the slain.

(vv. 66–68)

The suspicion of parody that shadows the epic dignity of
Jove opens to the threefold pride of Alexander. Yet neither of them is merely burlesqued: the myth, if a bit
pompous, is heroic; and even a hero sometimes may be a
little foolish. Here, as in the whole poem, the claims of
music, wine, war, and love are not denied: they are put
in their places with the good humor of a departing guest
at the world's feast.

DRYDEN'S TRANSLATION OF *Veni, Creator Spiritus* illustrates a remark of Dryden's quoted in the first chapter:
"By the harmony of words we elevate the mind to a sense

of devotion, as our solemn music, which is inarticulate poesy, does in churches." [5]

The primary work of harmony in *Veni, Creator Spiritus* is to establish a reverent and dignified tone, though there are also some more particular accommodations of sense and sound, as Dryden emulates, unfolds, and develops themes from the early medieval Latin hymn, only twenty-four lines long.[6]

> Creator Spirit, by whose aid
> The World's Foundations first were laid,
> Come visit ev'ry pious Mind;
> Come pour thy Joys on Human Kind:
> From Sin, and Sorrow set us free;   5
> And make thy Temples worthy Thee.
>
> O, Source of uncreated Light,
> The Father's promis'd *Paraclite!*
> Thrice Holy Fount, thrice Holy Fire,
> Our Hearts with Heav'nly Love inspire;   10
> Come, and thy Sacred Unction bring
> To Sanctifie us, while we sing!
>
> Plenteous of Grace, descend from high,
> Rich in thy sev'n-fold Energy!
> Thou strength of his Almighty Hand,   15
> Whose Pow'r does Heav'n and Earth command:
> Proceeding Spirit, our Defence,
> Who do'st the Gift of Tongues dispence,
> And crown'st thy Gift, with Eloquence!
>
> Refine and purge our Earthy Parts;   20
> But, oh, inflame and fire our Hearts!
> Our Frailties help, our Vice controul;
> Submit the Senses to the Soul;
> And when Rebellious they are grown,
> Then, lay thy hand, and hold 'em down.   25

Chace from our Minds th' Infernal Foe;
And Peace, the fruit of Love, bestow:
And, lest our Feet shou'd step astray,
Protect, and guide us in the way.

Make us Eternal Truths receive,   30
And practise, all that we believe:
Give us thy self, that we may see
The Father and the Son, by thee.

Immortal Honour, endless Fame
Attend th' Almighty Father's Name: 35
The Saviour Son, be glorify'd,
Who for lost Man's Redemption dy'd:
And equal Adoration be
Eternal *Paraclete*, to thee.

The form, the octosyllabic couplet, offers peculiar difficulties. To keep syntax untangled and diction clean without forcing rhyme or sense or meter requires great skill. Working the eight-syllable verse, says Dryden, "makes a poet giddy with turning in a space too narrow for his imagination." [7] (In fact, the primary joke of Hudibrastics is the *failure* to solve the problem, shown by the use of preposterous rhyme, metrics, and diction which convey contempt for the subject.)

Here the problem is solved with somber and reverent dignity. The basic pattern Dryden sets approaches a chant: four strong syllables in iambic rhythm to the verse, with five strong syllables in some verses, and six in "Thrice Holy Fount, thrice Holy Fire." (By "strong" I mean actually strong, whether or not metrically stressed.) Yet he varies that strong pattern in striking ways, varying feeling within the convention of religious awe. The general movement is slow, with numerous links of sound and words. Against that slow progress, little moments of speed or change make some lovely countermelodies.

In the first stanza, the norm approaches the pattern of the sixth verse, where "make," "Temp," "worth," and "Thee" are all strongly and about equally accented, as well as closely parallel in quantity and speed. Verses three and four each begin with the same strong unaccented syllable "Come," which is longer and richer but distinctly less accented than the accented syllable. There are at least four heavy accents in every verse, except for verses one and five. In verse one, the lightness of "by" is compensated for by the relatively heavy and long, though technically unaccented, "whose" and by the climactic progress of the last four syllables, which rise through four distinct degrees of accent: "it, by whose aid." In verse five, "set," though somewhat lighter than the other three accented syllables, receives some force from the strongly felt base and from the alliteration in the closely linked line: "*From Sin, and Sorrow set us free.*"

"O, Source" of verse seven shows an important reason why poets have found "O" of service: it slides its exclamatory force smoothly forward to a word at once rich in sound and profound in meaning. The power of the base and the slowing by convention and meaning strengthens the stressed syllables on "*uncreated*" to a prominence appropriate to their meaning and to the tremendous ontological excitement Dryden's best religious and moral poetry can convey.

"Thrice Holy Fount, thrice Holy Fire" is one of the most beautiful lines of our poetry, holding the six strong syllables (the most in any verse of the poem) in a liquid brilliance of movement and a double threeness of meter and meaning. Even the alliteration speaks, the *h*'s of "Holy" and "Holy" and "Heav'nly" converging on the "Hearts" of the following line even as the prayer asks for holiness to touch the heart. The *s*'s of the next several lines are equally binding, centering on the "Plenteous of Grace," in which both quantity and stress offer a plenitude of power.

Verses 18–19, by rhyme, by repetition of "Gift," and perhaps by some parallel precision of quantity of "Tongues" and "crown'st," knit together the special biblical gift of tongues and the continuing and illuminating eloquence of high Christian rhetoric and art (such as this poem).

In the first twenty verses, pauses are absent, light, or medial. Against that pattern, the second syllable of the twenty-first verse, with a pause before and after "oh," conveys and strengthens the *change* to personal and surging passion: "But, oh, inflame and fire our Hearts!"

The following verses are quieter, yet keep a steady dignity, sufficiently varied. The prayer to the Trinity intensifies to the remarkable and crucial verse thirty-seven: "Who for lost Man's Redemption dy'd." The pull of the norm of level accent is strong enough, almost, to make "lost man's" a real spondee, though I feel it remains a very strong trochee. It is the only place in the poem a trochee succeeds a trochee, and I find the verse indescribably strange and extremely moving. The lost is found. The last two verses lighten to an exact definition of dignity.

Through such patterning and variation, Dryden attains "the massive resonance" that Saintsbury so much admires.[8] That resonance is proper to the subject and to

132

the occasion; and the effect of massive resonance is increased by the importance and dignity of the subject. Translation though it is, the poem, in its freedom of emulation and its depth of feeling, earns a full right to be called one of the greatest English religious poems.

'A SONG FOR ST. CECILIA'S DAY' is an imperfect poem.[9] Compared to *Alexander's Feast*, it lacks energy and elaboration; compared to *Veni, Creator Spiritus*, it lacks consistency of tone. But section by section it is brilliant; [10] it reaches a grandeur that *Alexander's Feast* does not attempt and encompasses a comparable range.

I

From Harmony, from heav'nly Harmony
    This universal Frame began.
  When Nature underneath a heap
    Of jarring Atomes lay,
    And cou'd not heave her Head,
The tuneful Voice was heard from high,
    Arise ye more than dead.
Then cold, and hot, and moist, and dry,
  In order to their stations leap,
    And MUSICK's pow'r obey.
From Harmony, from heav'nly Harmony
    This universal Frame began:
    From Harmony to Harmony
Through all the compass of the Notes it ran,
The Diapason closing full in Man.

II

What Passion cannot MUSICK raise and quell!
  When *Jubal* struck the corded Shell,

133

His list'ning Brethren stood around
And wond'ring, on their Faces fell
To worship that Celestial Sound.
Less than a God they thought there cou'd not dwell
    Within the hollow of that Shell
    That spoke so sweetly and so well.
What Passion cannot MUSICK raise and quell!

III

The TRUMPETS loud Clangor
    Excites us to Arms
With shrill Notes of Anger
    And mortal Alarms.
That double double double beat
    Of the thundring DRUM
Cryes, heark the Foes come;
Charge, Charge, 'tis too late to retreat.

IV

The soft complaining FLUTE
In dying Notes discovers
The Woes of hopeless Lovers,
Whose Dirge is whisper'd by the warbling LUTE.

V

Sharp VIOLINS proclaim
Their jealous Pangs, and Desperation,
Fury, frantick Indignation,
Depth of Pains, and height of Passion,
    For the fair, disdainful Dame.

VI

But oh! what Art can teach
What human Voice can reach
The sacred ORGANS praise?
Notes inspiring holy Love,

134

> Notes that wing their heav'nly ways
> To mend the Choires above.

VII

> *Orpheus* cou'd lead the savage race;
> And Trees unrooted left their place;
>   Sequacious of the Lyre:
> But bright CECILIA rais'd the wonder high'r;
> When to her ORGAN, vocal Breath was giv'n
> An Angel heard, and straight appear'd
>   Mistaking Earth for Heaven.

Grand CHORUS

> *As from the pow'r of sacred Lays*
>   *The Spheres began to move,*
> *And sung the great Creator's praise*
>   *To all the bless'd above;*
> *So when the last and dreadful hour*
> *This crumbling Pageant shall devour,*
> *The TRUMPET shall be heard on high,*
> *The Dead shall live, the Living die,*
> *And MUSICK shall untune the Sky.*

The defects of tone come partly from the facility of the musical imitations,[11] and partly from ambiguous qualities in the St. Cecilia legend. To be overtly conscious of one's medium is always dangerously to approach the incongruous; Dryden's brilliant imitations of the qualities of different musical instruments awake comic or at least trivializing potentialities which he apparently did not recognize. In *Alexander's Feast* he was to solve that peculiar problem by the magnificently good-natured convention of slightly ironic appraisal that governs much of the poem. Here he did not solve it; the poem is marred by uncertainty of tone.

But, if he fails to achieve the mastery of tone of *Alexander's Feast*, he reaches heights not permitted to that poem. Verrall's description of the assumption of *A Song for St. Cecilia's Day* is admirable: "The theory of . . . Dryden is that the world was created, and is held together, by harmony—that is, proportion—and that man, the microcosm, is a summary of creation, responsive to all rhythms." [12]

The theory provides the structure of the poem. In the first section, creation occurs by harmony. The Christian idea of creation is mixed with Lucretian and pre-Socratic atomism and Neoplatonic or Pythagorean numerology. [13] Nature, oddly, exists even in the chaos before creation. Dryden would hardly subscribe to such an idea outside the poem, but he makes good use of it in dramatizing the creation. As in Milton, nature stands for the potentiality of nature. Music rescues nature from chaos. It is not clear whether the "tuneful Voice" is Music's or God's; the syntax suggests that it is Music's. Either way, Music is the voice of God. The diapason closes in man; [14] since it does, music (and poetry) are possible. The following sections show something of the variety of the nature to which man responds and which provides for the possibility of good music or poetry. Poetry can imitate music, music, the passions, and the passions can respond with propriety to the various realities of the world, a response made possible by accords fixed in nature and man by the creation. Fixed, but not frozen. It is a vital world.

The first section is about creation; the next six are about nature as reflected by music; the Grand Chorus is about the Last Judgment. The order of the whole is world history, though the central sections are not historical. The second is about the power of Music over the passions in general; the third, war and its proper instrument the drum; the fourth and fifth, soft and more passionate human love as rendered by the flute (and lute) and the violin respectively; the sixth, holy love and the organ. The seventh section, odd as it is,[15] serves as a kind of summary, Orpheus representing the power of natural (secular) music, St. Cecilia representing the higher power of supernatural (sacred) music.

The structure has two flaws. First, the central sections are neither chronological nor providential and hence fail to provide an adequate transition from creation to Judgment. Second, those sections are too thin, thin in tone and in size, for the beginning and ending. Imposing pillars are joined by a tenuous thread.

Section by section, the poem is very fine. The imitative versification, which displays brilliant virtuosity in the middle sections, is less obvious and more splendid in the sections on Creation and Judgment. Verrall has said that this section involves a recognition of the fact that purely irregular Pindarics are proper to nothing but chaos, the delayed rhyme of "Harmony" with "Harmony" representing the triumph of harmony over chaos.

One view of the syllabic count and rhyme scheme attests to the truth of Verrall's remark.[16]

Verse	Syllables	Rhyme
1	10	a
2	8	b
3	8	c
4	6	d
5	6	e
6	8	a
7	6	e

Verse	Syllables	Rhyme
8	8	a
9	8	c
10	6	d
11	10	a
12	8	b
13	8	a
14	10	b
15	10	b

The last five verses make a clearly comprehensible stanzaic pattern, realizing the harmony that the first ten verses are seeking. In those ten verses, syllabic and rhyme patterning, in keeping with the meaning, represent a struggle of starts and stops, progresses and rebuffs, a struggle toward harmony. Verses 11 and 12 repeat verses 1 and 2 and signal the resolution.

Even with the semichaos of the first ten verses, the variations are skillful, for the most part opening and closing the pattern as the meaning opens and closes. The full verse of the opening narrows first to eight syllables and then to six as we see nature entrapped. Nature reaches her worse plight in the short, "jarring," apparently rhymeless verses 4 and 5. The next two verses, signaling escape from bondage, open out to a common meter and satisfy the ear with the first true rhymes in the poem. "Arise" is an imitative word, the second syllable lifting sharply from the very light first in accent, quantity, and pitch. The four elements exist in level and slow metrical and syntactical parallelism, moving to order through the considerable commotion of verse 9, where the firm word "order" stands against the rush to the "stations." "And MUSICK's pow'r obey," a firm and equally stressed verse, closes out the section in meaning, "obey" ending the distant and involved rhyming of the first ten verses. Against that background in which chaos is seen coming to harmony, the last five verses present a full-throated, happy, and assured harmony of nature and man.

Section I ends with a heroic couplet. Section II almost begins with one (5a 4a) and almost, in reverse, ends with one (4a 5a). It is a demonstration of rhyming, of pure metrical energy purifying itself as it goes, of opening and closing, of making a stanza form from the couplet's impact of exact energies and strong rhyme. The pattern is the following:

Number of feet in line	Rhyme scheme
5	a
4	a
4	b
4	a
4	b
5	a
4	a
4	a
5	a

Almost too brilliant, it remains lovely, appropriately lesser than the opening section. Section I moves from the *musica mundana* to the *musica humana*[17] which echoes that echo of the divine. Section II moves, as *musica humana* ("which unites the incorporeal activity of the reason with the body," according to Boethius)[18] and thus as transition to the lesser *musica instrumentalis* of the imitations of sections III, IV, and V.

Those sections, delightful as they are, are too thin, too out of keeping with the grandeur of the poem's opening and close; and section VII with its curiously bright, Renaissance-painterly note [19] is to me—with the best will and historical imagination I can offer—finally only quaint. But one cannot deny the excellence of the transition. In section VI, Dryden turns from his imitations to the nobly inimitable, the quietness of his motion suggesting the humility of his "Notes" which, even so, reflect and partake of something of the heavenly.

The heavenly is also the awful; and Dryden poses against the soaring harmony of the poem's opening the devout and awe-struck warning of the Grand Chorus.

> *As from the pow'r of sacred Lays*   55
>   *The Spheres began to move,*
> *And sung the great Creator's praise*
>   *To all the bless'd above:*
> *So when the last and dreadful hour*
> *This crumbling Pageant shall devour,*   60
> *The* TRUMPET *shall be heard on high,*
> *The Dead shall live, the Living die,*
> *And* MUSICK *shall untune the Sky.*

Imitative harmony is less important here, but real. The change of form (from the common measure quatrain to the couplet to the triplet) represents contrast strongly felt. The "quatrain" of lines 55–58 is smooth, flowing: the last lines give off resonance as solemn [20] as the tetrameters of *Veni, Creator Spiritus.*

The imagery and syntax are no less solemn. The inversion in *"So when the last and dreadful hour / This crumbling Pageant shall devour,"* even though the meaning is clear, gives "devour" a strange force (as though the word were intransitive); which strengthens the relations, multiple and perturbing, of "hour," "devour," and "crumbling." The words "crumbling" and "devour" give a grotesque physical significance to the line: the world is being eaten; yet it is the abstract and invisible "hour" that devours it. A world passes into nothingness in the very structure of the image. *"The Dead shall live, the Living die,"* may appear an obvious paradox, but it is not. Both of the statements are to Dryden physically true, for at the last judgment the dead shall be raised and the living shall pass over into eternity; the verse sets up reverberations of terror responsive to the many and fearful relations between physical and spiritual deaths and lives. The last verse is the best in the poem. The curious accentuation of "untune" flavors the unresolved sound of the line. The word "untune" is one of the many in seventeenth-century language which has alternative stress.[21] The contrast recommends "un" for stress; the meter recommends "tune." The untuning is a reversal of the grand harmonic processes of the Creation; it is also, in sound and meaning, the sudden relaxing of a taut string. It is, as it is meant to be, an unsettling line. Order almost visibly drops toward chaos, the music of the spheres toward an awful silence, a silence the poem comes to share.

8

The Maze of Death:
All for Love

'ALL FOR LOVE' is a pale, beautiful play. A steady quietness prevails in and under it. The brilliant plot, the varied yet strongly felt morality, the characters who strangely loom into individual poetic substance within the frames of their typicality, the warm and lucid imagery,[1] the near or utter perfection of the resolving and changing cadency of the meters, all exist in a dreamlike quiet where action comes to rest. The smaller and larger rhythms and structure move in a unity.

The unity persists through and blends the tones. The tones, sharply different to analysis, do not seem so in the actual motioning of the play. The verse often sounds clear and briskly managed, yet a romantic light lights the play. "Who dreamed that beauty passes like a dream?" Dryden as well as Yeats did, particularly in some dreamlike passages, such as the following speech of Antony's:

142

> *Antony.*   How I lov'd
> Witness ye Dayes and Nights, and all your hours,
> That Danc'd away with Down upon your Feet,
> As all your bus'ness were to count my passion.
> One day past by, and nothing saw but Love;
> Another came, and still 'twas only Love:
> The Suns were weary'd out with looking on,
> And I untyr'd with loving.
> I saw you ev'ry day, and all the day;
> And ev'ry day was still but as the first:
> So eager was I still to see you more.
>
> (2.281b–91)[2]

Slow syllables, rich and long, linked in sound, moving toward equal timing, lingered over in the pronouncing, frequently ending in or including *m*'s or *n*'s or *s*'s or *r*'s, repeated and turned about, name qualities which their rhythms enter. The words Dryden conjures with are "hours," "danced," "count," "passed," "wearied." The time pattern makes a sort of supertemporal stasis of the movement of time:[3] Antony addresses the very times which are dancing away, and the suns are transcended; normal time does not measure. The *still* joins meanings ("even yet" or "even then" and "always") to make a time which is eternal, not-of-time, as well as the present time of his present and poignant memories. The transcendence, mostly rant, of the heroic plays moves to a gentler and more persuasive music.

The motion is smooth; the times tend to equality (which fits the meaning: all times are one). In reading, one tends to linger out the quantities. The turns on the language turn within the melody. No diction obtrudes except for the slight emerging of *business* and *passion*, trochaic words ending phrases in an iambic line, whose identity and opposition of meaning are crossed and supporting strands in the moral net of the play. All flows, dreamlike, into the romantic dream, time and death flow to the lover's measures.

Yet Antony is rejecting Cleopatra. The speech is a gloss on his stern "And hid me from the bus'ness of the World / . . . To give whole years to you" (2.278, 280), but Antony is half-trapped, more than half mesmerized, by the world-dissolving rhythms of the memories which he is, he thinks, honorably putting by.

One of the play's greatest verses comes shortly after (2.296), and partakes its uncertain shares of bitter recriminations and the lover's dream, in the almost tranced passivity of Antony's melancholy humor. "The World fell mouldring from my hands each hour." The three clustered strong syllables (second, third, and fourth) express the slowness as the three light syllables in a row are mimetic of the crumbling. The "hour" and the "World" turn on the title and the previous speech. The "World" and "mould" are heavy of kinship in sound and identify each other, what his action and inaction are in their postponed resemblance. The verse is another excellent example of significant variation from a recognized base.

| The   World | fell   mould | ring || from | my   hands |
each hour. | i I *i* i I

The quality of the speech and the structure of the scene seem unsuited, since the debate is a sharp turn in the play's brisk action. Yet the meeting of briskness and dream-haunting is as essential to the play's action as to its themes. For, had not Antony been so haunted, he would not have turned from duty to Cleopatra, and there would be no story. There is a story, a rapid one, of which Dryden in the Preface says, "The action is . . . one, . . . every scene in the tragedy conducing to the main design, and every act concluding with a turn of it" (Watson, I, *222*).

The plot has been frequently praised,[4] though sometimes with the suggestion that the play really lives, not in its action, but in the quality of its poetry. But the meeting of the plot with the poetry (in normal and in special ways) is an integral part of the full design, and necessary to an understanding of the true merit of the poetry.

Despair begins the play. The disastrous defeat at Actium has left no reasonable hope for military success; Cleopatra has left Antony; Octavia solicits revenge; the Roman armies approach; and Antony retreats into a profoundly melancholy dream. The first verb used of Antony is "dream"; the first three verbs he uses of himself are passives; the first metaphor he offers reduces him to a passively determined if illustrious body.[5] Even his famous lines of remembered triumph (1.297–304) are essentially passive. The mood, gentle or awful in its darkness, recurs (as an undernote never leaves), yet the action goes its prompt way. One is apt to get a sort of impression that Antony is not so much vacillating as simply passive and pushed to and fro;[6] yet he makes important decisions, on evidence of some weight.

Ventidius sympathizes with his despairing mood, but persuades him to rejoin the war, using not only appeals to honor, friendship, and responsibility but the solid fact that there are in Syria twelve loyal and able legions willing to fight under Antony's command. Even the debate they have over Cleopatra is set into actuality by another military fact: the legions will not fight for her.

The next turn for Antony is back to Cleopatra, but it is not a mere swaying in a vain wind. Once again there occurs persuasive argument, which appeals to the nostalgia of love. Also, Cleopatra proves that she has refused an offer by Octavius to give her Egypt and Syria if she will desert Antony and ally her troops with Octavius'. He turns his loyalty back to the faithful Cleopatra, *and* goes out to battle, thus, to his mind, acting on the evidence and being loyal to Ventidius, Cleopatra, and himself.

The third act, which begins with Antony returning victorious from the fray, introduces the Dolabella episodes. It is not Antony's weakness which brings Dolabella, but Ventidius' hardheaded military prudence. Ventidius suggests an honorable negotiated peace as the most rational military step. When Antony replies that such a peace is not possible, Ventidius recommends that Antony seek out a friend in Octavius' confidence who might persuade Octavius to negotiate. Dolabella is the obvious candidate, though Antony has some misgivings because he fears that Dolabella's suspected infatuation for Cleopatra may have marred his friendship toward Antony. Thus Dryden, at once, has prepared the way for the later turns of mutual jealousy, has given a reason for Dolabella to be sought out, and has shown Antony making an apparently wise choice under the rational, strategically sound advice of Ventidius. Dolabella arrives with Octavia, who is a natural person to help in the negotiations because she can appeal at once to Antony's sense of honor and familial duty and love, and also to his mili-

146

tary prudence. The scene which follows between Octavia and Cleopatra—though in its way lively—does lower the dignity of the play [7] and, as William Archer sees correctly as more important,[8] does not contribute to the progress of the action. Though Antony's reconcilement to Octavia is too abrupt, as critics have often felt,[9] it is supported by sensible reflection on the situation and Antony's deep attachment to his family and his honor.

So far in the play, each decision which Antony has made depends not only on moral and emotional appeals, but also on relevant and important information which Antony comes to know: (1) there are twelve loyal legions; (2) Cleopatra has refused an offer which would save her, in order to be true to Antony; (3) rational negotiations are possible.

In act IV, deceptions begin to weave their own defeat.[10] Antony asks Dolabella to inform Cleopatra that Antony is permanently leaving her. Dolabella exhibits a struggle between love and friendship, is overheard by Ventidius, who hopes that events may develop so that Antony's rage at Cleopatra's fickleness may sever the last bond. Alexas, more expert at such intrigues, sees a chance to bring Antony back to Cleopatra by jealousy. Cleopatra is too straightforward to wish to do so, but in desperation forces herself to make the attempt. She flirts with Dolabella who by the force of his passion is driven to a lie (that Antony was in a fury of cold hatred when he pronounced the harsh words). They both rapidly repent, and it is in their confessing their deceptions to each other that they make it possible for Octavia and Ventidius to find evidence of a guilty love. When they report to Antony, his paroxysm of jealousy is the final straw for Octavia: she leaves him. Here the choice is not Antony's. Not once in the play has he been moved to an important change by purely emotional suasion: the plot is deliberative and highly causative.

Act V unfolds what has been established. Alexas' lie about Cleopatra's suicide leads to Antony's suicide, which leads to Cleopatra's real suicide, which leads to a ritual of marriage and the final words of the play. Thus they evade and transcend Octavius Caesar, and the ritual, with its hints of coronation, military victory, and marriage, takes the place of deliberative action and leads to the closing words.

The plot is satisfying, almost in effect contradictory. There is the sense of despair, the moving steadily and gravely forward toward the fatal conclusion; there is the to-and-fro of the turns in Antony's mind, the emotional shiftings of allegiance and hopes; there is the complex and deliberative plotting I have traced (plot is not all, but surely the modern lack of appreciation of firm plotting is blind); there is the curiously rational calm of the lucidly drawn issues; there is the mysterious and pervasive romantic quietness which moves among all these. The causation involved has a richness and irreducibility at least analogous to that of actual human causation, and which, like the causation and freedom we experience and infer, slides through our categories and escapes. To put it a different way, the representation and the action represented (*mimesis* and *praxis*) are richer than a given schematization of them, including the mixed one I am engaged in making in this essay. The whole power of the total rhythm inheres within the richness of the play.

If one means by "plot" or "action" the whole plot or

action, one means the play, every word and gesture. If one means by plot any given, however cunning, selection of incidents, one is selecting, and in the process ignoring connections. If one lists the action of the play, gives what we call a plot summary, one leaves out much which the reader of the summary infers or guesses at (such as the motives which cause the action) and a great deal which is structural which the reader of a plot summary cannot infer or sensibly guess at. The structure of incidents is not a heap of incidents. Move away from any given reduction, and one is on the road to tautology: the play is the thing of the play. Wholes are wholes, not parts. But merely to stress the whole (however lyric the declamation may become) is to miss much which does contribute to our real sense of structure, for instance the plot in a rough ordinary sense of the word. We can think about, though we cannot truly define, what goes into the total rhythm of a work of art.

Part of that total rhythm in *All for Love* is the moral causes and implications within the play. The morality is perturbed; it is confusing; it is on the face of things manifestly self-inconsistent; [11] yet it is of the motion and the shaping of the play, and it has its lucidities.

The title is *All for Love or the World Well Lost*. Yet Dryden writes in the Preface that the attraction of the subject for him was "the excellency of the moral. For the chief persons represented were famous patterns of unlawful love; and their end accordingly was unfortunate." [12]

The contradiction is as blunt as may be: the world is *well* lost; their love is fully justified; yet the author approves their punishment. There is no reason to doubt the sincerity of either assertion. Dryden goes on to offer a sober, if simplified, theory of the place of morality in the play:

> All reasonable men have long since concluded that the hero of the poem ought not to be a character of perfect virtue, for then he could not, without injustice, be made unhappy; nor yet altogether wicked, because he could not then be pitied. I have therefore steered the middle course; and have drawn the character of Antony as favourably as Plutarch, Appian, and Dion Cassius would give me leave; the like I have observed in Cleopatra. That which is wanting to work up the pity to a greater height, was not afforded me by the story; for the crimes of love, which they both committed were not occasioned by any necessity, or fatal ignorance, but were wholly voluntary; since our passions are, or ought to be, within our power.

That view contradicts both the title and the "Imperial Triumph" (5.515) of the conclusion, but it is seriously given. Dryden was not the first or the last human being to say some confused things about sexual morality. His confusion enters the mixing and the strengths of the play.

The notion of poetic justice expressed in "their end accordingly was unfortunate" is apt to be pushed aside with some contempt, a contempt a little too automatic. Poetic justice is a partial notion, and its share in the crime of "improving" Shakespeare is as gross as well known. Still, there is something to it. If Cordelia does come to grief, so do Edmund, and Regan, and Goneril; and justice does triumph in the state, in *Macbeth* and *Hamlet* as in *King Lear*. From Aristotle on, the question

of moral justice is germane to tragedy, however narrow
or insipid the abuses of the idea. In some deep way a
great work of art should satisfy, in truth, in beauty, and
in justice; and should somehow reconcile the three. It
should, in Yeats's great phrase, "hold in a single thought
reality and justice."

There are two solid objections to the abuse of "poetic
justice": endings where good and evil are plainly rewarded and punished are apt to go contrary to our sense
of what is likely to happen (our sense of probability,
verisimilitude), and also—what is less often mentioned
and may be more important—to frustrate our desire for
adequate causation. We want plays to carry through,
from impulses and motives, by agents. Rewards and punishments not distributed by those agents or not flowing
from the natural consequence of actions, cross our
sense of causality. If, for instance, they occur by apparent chance or are handed out by a human or divine
referee, not a genuine party to the issuing action, we feel
a break in the design. However, not all rewards and
punishments are unfunctional. Macduff kills Macbeth;
that is punishment, but also sequence. Or, to take an
example of a sort Dryden develops here, a deception
which turns back on the deceiver satisfies three relevant
desires of an audience: that causation be consecutive,
that an action have a unifying shape, and that the moral
sense be not thwarted. Evil does frequently, in fact and
not merely in hoping, block or destroy itself. Good often
fails, but often works through. To deny those truths in
art can cross our sense of development and probability
as surely as a happy ending got by dramatically unper-
suasive means.

The moral notions of the Preface in part work out in

the play, and in part do not. On the face of it, Dryden
fails to reach his end: the lovers should end, he has told
us, unfortunately. Yet they escape Octavius and achieve
"Spousals" (5.461) and triumph and long-lasting earthly
fame. However, in a different way, which the Dryden of
the Preface does not admit, but the Dryden of the play
and title does, those "Spousals" are poetic justice; their
great and noble love should be and is rewarded. Two
notions of value conflict. Love counters responsibility,
and both by the tragic-triumphant ending get something
of what is due. Since the love is unlawful, the lovers lose
(die); since their love is great, they win (triumph in
death).

This is, one feels, a trifle schematic compared to the
profoundest sense of reconciliation in the greatest tragedies. The worlds are not as powerfully and mysteriously
opposite as they might be: there is too much clear
"Roman" and Corneillian reasoning and fidelity and, yes,
even innocence in their love.

At least three other moral themes and categories appear, and mix, or do not mix. First, the structural elements of morality touched on in my discussion of plot,
especially the love-friendship-honor conflicts, and the
web of deceit. Those conflicts are not simply occasions
for standard Love-Honor debates, like those of the heroic plays, though they develop from them.[13] The pulls
are more various: friendship struggling against honor as
well as against love. Nor are the pairings as tidy, or as
tidily confused, as the noble-guilty pairing is at times.
For instance, Octavius is tried and found wanting, not
because he does not understand romantic love, but for
strong Roman reasons (especially, in 2.110–18, the turn

on chance and virtue sounding a major note); and on one occasion of lovely rationalizing Antony gives his devotion to Roman customs as his reason for seeing Cleopatra (2.230–33). Second, the heroic drama claptrap (too courteous a word) about the ego above destiny (1.406–11a, 2.20–22). In Dryden's defense it needs to be said that such a "morality" is surprisingly rare considering how much of it there had been—and was to be again—in his other plays.[14] A third category, evinced in a speech in which Dolabella asks mercy, has some structural hints.

> Heav'n has but
> Our sorrow for our sins; and then delights
> To pardon erring Man: sweet Mercy seems
> Its darling Attribute, which limits Justice;
> As if there were degrees in Infinite,
> And Infinite would rather want perfection
> Than punish to extent.
>
> (4.539b–45a)

The first clause seems to me ambiguous. "Heaven no sooner receives our sorrow, penitence, than it hastens to forgive." Or perhaps "Heaven, being perfect and without passions, has no sorrow for our sin except our own, which Heaven takes into itself as payment, and then delights to forgive." The rest of the speech says that it seems almost as though God would rather mete out too little justice than not express his loving mercy toward men. But the "as if" is important. There are no degrees in God's infinitude, and He is fully just and fully loving in ways which reconcile our struggles and exceed our wit. Justice and mercy are, beyond us, one. Antony, by refus-

153

ing the mercy asked for, takes a long step toward his final defeat. The "mercy" he refuses to offer would really be justice, since Dolabella and Cleopatra have not betrayed him, a complication which adds a structural tightening of the web. Later, Charmion (5.1–4) sees Antony's unjust and merciless treatment of Dolabella and Cleopatra as evidence for atheism. If justice fails, randomness must rule. But that is not the last word.

The moral workings are dense, aslant, functional, imperfect. The metrical shapings are at Dryden's disposal from the first speech of the play.

> *Serapion.* Portents and Prodigies, are grown so frequent,
> That they have lost their Name. Our fruitful *Nile*
> Flow'd ere the wonted Season, with a Torrent
> So unexpected, and so wondrous fierce,
> That the wild Deluge overtook the haste
> Ev'n of the Hinds that watch'd it: Men and Beasts
> Were born above the tops of trees, that grew
> On th'utmost Margin of the Water-mark.
> Then, with so swift an Ebb, the Floud drove backward
> It slipt from underneath the Scaly Herd:
> Here monstrous *Phocae* panted on the shore;
> Forsaken *Dolphins* there, with their broad tails,
> Lay lashing the departing Waves: Hard by 'em,
> Sea-Horses floundring in the slimy mud,
> Toss'd up their heads, and dash'd the ooze about 'em.
>   (1.1–15)

The crowding-toward of accents in verse 8 brings the margin and the mark to neighborhood. Stresses heap to power in verse 9. The "Scaly Herd" is a specimen of neoclassical diction, for once valid by being monstrous, as is the word *"Phocae,"* freakish in tone and lighter in sound than the heavy and linked "monstrous" and "panted." "Lay lashing" and "floundring" and "slimy mud" are for the mouth as well as for the ear to linger and thicken, and enjoy; and line 15 springs the "toss'd up" and "dash'd" to the "ooze" with an energy which speaks gayness in the midst of horror. *Ooze* belongs to a class of words (*sparkles* also belongs) in which the shape of sound mimics the form of a perception of a different sense (with *ooze*, sight and whatever sense—it is not simply touch—recognizes motion in time and shape against the hand). The horror of the passage is theatrical. This Dryden—he is an old friend—delights us by showing off. Another and profounder Dryden controls most of the play. *His* first image, a fully serious image of power and danger, opens the true action.

> All Southern, from yon hills, the *Roman* camp
> Hangs o'er us black and threatning, like a Storm
> Just breaking on our heads.
>
> (1.42–44)

The richness of cadency, pressure, and balance of strong words and strong things narrows with the last verse of the speech (the third hemistich in the play) to the concentrated force of the threat. The clear yet mellow and resonant imagery which blooms throughout the play owes some of its reality to the cadency which gives the exact measure of what a metaphor imports.

Rhythm is the interplay of repetitions and changes. Secondary patterns of rhythm may come from almost any poetic element capable of intentness and repeating;

and counterpatternings can work on and against each other and against the hinted, known, felt, unheard metrical form behind the sound.

One of the most important kinds of secondary pattern is phrasal: phrases or words can be repeated, the ends of phrases can come in various places in the verses, and the metrical shape of phrases can be felt as counterpatterns within the sound. Good examples occur in the speech in which Alexas introduces Ventidius to the audience. It is proper that Alexas gives the first and most definitive statement of his enemy and counterpart.

> But, let me witness to the worth I hate,
> A braver Roman never drew a Sword.
> Firm to his Prince; but, as a friend, not slave.
> He ne'r was of his pleasures; but presides
> O're all his cooler hours and morning counsels:
> In short, the plainness, fierceness, rugged virtue
> Of an old true-stampt Roman lives in him.
>
> (1.100–106)

Verse 101 comes close to the iambic base: light stresses light, heavy stresses heavy, quantity and isochronism tending to reinforce the stress pattern. In verse 102, the important words set off by the metrical patterning define the relation: firm   prince   friend. In verse 103 "pleasures" and "presides" have enough likeness to enforce a contrast. The "cooler hours" and "morning counsels" have the same rhetorical and metrical shape, trochaic adjective followed by trochaic noun within a straight iambic movement. The trochaic words of line 105 counter exactly the iambic movement of the line and speak their meaning firmly. Trochaic words in iambic rhythm are one of the commonest features of English verse, but seldom so pronounced and definitive as in this example. The four clustered successive stresses of verse 106 of "old true-stampt Ro" tell what they are. This is *writing*, with Dryden in charge, but it is to me a highly gratifying kind of writing, fancy exalted by will to imagination's door. Dryden wrote once that "Poesy must resemble natural truth, but it must *be* ethical." In this passage the sound-sense-phrase-meter patterns are morally defining.

Ventidius, in one of his first speeches to Alexas, makes a profound and obscene definition of what Alexas' queen, supported by Alexas' crooking counsel, has done to Antony. Not here "firm prince friend"!

> Oh, she has deck'd his ruin with her love,
> Led him in golden bands to gaudy slaughter,
> And made perdition pleasing: She has left him
> The blank of what he was;
> I tell thee, Eunuch, she has quite unman'd him:
> Can any *Roman* see, and know him now,
> Thus alter'd from the Lord of half Mankind,
> Unbent, unsinew'd, made a Woman's Toy,
> Shrunk from the vast extent of all his honors,
> And crampt within a corner of the World?
> O, *Antony!*
> Thou bravest Soldier, and thou best of Friends!
> (1.170–81)

Verse 171 is one more example of the common pattern of a straight falling rhythm in an iambic line. In movement, and in a correct scansion out of the iambic context, the line is dtttt, but it scans in context tiiii<. The "golden bands" and "gaudy slaughter" parallel each other's movement and are severally linked in sound. The bands are ornaments, are an emblem of love, are bonds.

157

The "gaudy slaughter"[15] is as voracious a name for female sexuality as fascinated anger might desire. The "blank" is "Eunuch" and "unman'd" because the sounds and stresses link.[16] The links are the more damning because of the fine rhetorical shaping of verse 174. The scansion is iiiii<. The rhetorical movement is btab. The amphibrachic counterpattern is one of the most supple in iambics, giving a vigor and stasis, a rocking forward. The "unman'd" holds what Ventidius considers the moral truth of the affair. Antony, and Dryden, respect his judgment. The rank pun is carried on by an extraordinarily forceful and related series of words: *unbent, unsinewed, shrunk, extent, cramped.* By exercising his virile manhood, Antony has become no man, when judged by the true standards of manhood, which are responsibility and just ambition. His fall from high responsibility and estate is, as plainly as metaphors can speak it, the subsiding of the penis after coition. Hence he is a eunuch, in actuality till he can perform the act again, and in reality because he is surrendering his manhood for mere sexuality. Yet he is, not was, "Thou bravest Soldier, and thou best of Friends!" Whatever happens, the two are one. The soldier is a friend. So the meters say, even though friendship and honor oppose, even though a friend is sunk from friendship's honor to dishonoring love. The relation stands. F. R. Leavis speaks, a little condescendingly, of the "ballet" of the action.[17] That ballet is reflected in little in such passages as this one, and it is too fine a ballet for anyone to condescend to.

One could add many and successful, and highly various, examples of the counterpatterning of rhetoric and meter throughout the play, within a sustaining tone. A particularly lovely one plays falling patterns against rising ones, a patterning itself counterpatterned by the play of half-verses.

> . . . Ingrateful Woman!
> Who follow'd me, but as the Swallow Summer,
> Hatching her young ones in my kindly Beams,
> Singing her flatt'ries to my morning wake;
> But, now my Winter comes, she spreads her wings,
> And seeks the spring of *Caesar.*
> *Alexas:* Think not so:
>
> (5.208–13b)

Dryden enjoyed the play of half-verses for the same reason he enjoyed spruce argument. The quick variety, the "chase of wit,"[18] seems to come naturally to his hand. Sometimes it works out into regular iambic verses, sometimes not. It does in 1.246–51. The shifts of argument and affection turn on each other, in astonishing loops of phrase and in plain iambics.

> A. Art thou *Ventidius?*   V. Are you *Antony?*
> I'm liker what I was, than you to him
> I left you last.   A. I'm angry.   V. So am I.
> A. I would be private: leave me.   V. Sir, I love you,
> And therefore will not leave you.   A. Will not leave me?
> Where have you learnt that Answer? Who am I?

Another example is found in 1.344–59 with normal iambic pentametric movement throughout. Verses 1.344–46 are stichomythia (5 speeches), followed by two

159

regular verses (347–48), followed by three more verses of stichomythia (349–51, 4 speeches), followed by a regular verse (352), followed by two more verses of stichomythia (353–54, 3 speeches), followed by three regular verses (355–57). After that variety (yet normality) verse 358 seems most clipped.

	Than yon trim Bands can buy.	} i i i i i
Antony.	Where left you them?	
Ventidius.	I said in Lower *Syria.*	} i i i i i <
Antony.	Bring 'em hither;	
	There may be life in these.	} i i i i i
Ventidius.	They will not come.	

Antony.   Why did'st thou mock my hopes with promis'd aids,
To double my despair? They'r mutinous.

Ventidius.	Most firm and loyal.	} i i i i i
Antony.	Yet they will not march	
	To succour me. Oh trifler!	} i i i i i <
Ventidius.	They petition	
	You would make hast to head 'em.	} i i i i i
Antony.	I'm besieg'd.	

Ventidius.   There's but one way shut up: How came I hither?

Antony.	I will not stir.	} i i i i i
Ventidius.	They would perhaps desire	
	A better reason.	} i i i i i
Antony.	I have never us'd	

My Soldiers to demand a reason of
My actions. Why did they refuse to
March?

Ventidius.   They said they would not fight for *Cleopatra.*

Antony.   What was't they said?

> *Ventidius.* They said, they would not fight for *Cleopatra.*
>
> (1.344–59)

The effect is remarkable, Dryden is at his brisk surest, and the verses offer one of several reasons inherent in the possibility of blank verse which led him to discover, at last, its superiority to the rhymed couplet as a dramatic medium. The last three verses show Dryden's fondness for turning music into and out of the name of Cleopatra, of which 3.450–58 is a lovely example, and the following verses the most important.

> *Antony.* What Woman was it, whom you heard and saw
> So playful with my Friend!
> > Not *Cleopatra?*
>
> *Ventidius.* Ev'n she, my lord.
> *Antony.* My *Cleopatra?*
> *Ventidius.* Your *Cleopatra;*
> *Dolabella's Cleopatra:*
> Every Man's *Cleopatra.*
> *Antony.* Thou ly'st.
> *Ventidius.* I do not lye, my Lord.
> Is this so strange? Should Mistresses be left,
> And not provide against a time of change?
> You know she's not much us'd to lonely nights.
>
> (4.293–304)

No scansion neatly works out, and none needs to. The break in the movement comes on the grand sneer of Ventidius's "Your," and even then the curious result approaches a double pentametric form.

| So play | ful with | my Friend! | Not *Cle* | *opat* |
                                  i *i* i I i

ra? Ev | 'n she | , my Lord! | My *Cle* | *opatra?*
                                     i i i T i <

| Your *Cle* | *opat* | *ra;* *Dol* | *abell* | *a's* *Cle* | *opat* | *ra;*
Eve | ry Man's | *Cleopatra.*[19]   t i i i i i i i t t

The real rhythm is rhetorical and dipodic not in the whole verses but in the key words:

$$\text{Cléopátra} \quad \text{Cléopátra} \quad \text{Cléopátra} \quad \text{Dólabélla's}$$
$$\text{Cléopátra} \quad \text{Évery Mán's} \quad \text{Cléopátra}$$

The departure comes back to cold and sober iambics, strengthened by the rhetorical reversal of the first foot: *I* do not lie, my lord. The next three verses restore the full rhythm of iambics and have some sadness in their irony, the rhyme (*strange—change*) stroking a light memory of the heroic couplets of Dryden's earlier plays which the blank verse has left happily behind. The departure and the return are alike brilliant, cold and hard irony against hurt numbness, both violating and sustained by the friendship which underlies and is not to fail.

Such are some of the sweetness and sustenances of the multifold rhythms of the play. Yet they do not show the unity of the play. No analysis does that. A play's unity is at last and at first its own. Love-death-time-love-dream. Of much, a dream. Partly the dream is a tone, and tone is what it is. Yet one may gesture at its appearances and its nature.

The speech I discussed first (2.281b–91) holds qualities

which persist throughout the play. Naturally enough the play is rich with references and images for melancholy and death, but what I speak of is stranger than that.

The first verb for Antony (1.47) is "dream." Cleopatra's last speech finds death a mist of numbing (5.493–501), the great speech shortly before finds death a slumber of a deceived image (5.473–79a). Early in the play, Cleopatra's birthday moves in a sort of otherness.

> *Alexas.* . . . Her own Birth-day
> Our Queen neglected, like a vulgar Fate,
> That pass'd obscurely by.
> *Ventidius.* Would it had slept,
> Divided far from his; till some remote
> And future Age had call'd it out, to ruin
> Some other Prince, not him.
> (1.160–65a)

The "Fate" joins birth and death, and high and low. That her birthday (compared to a fate) might sleep gives another note than Ventidius's hostile meaning. As though things slept in causes and fate fed on dreaming.

At the end of the first act, Antony, in a metaphor which opposes yet moves within those themes, celebrates his new vow to lead his troops.

> Come on, My Soldier!
> Our hearts and armes are still the same: I long
> Once more to meet our foes; that Thou and I,
> Like Time and Death, marching before our Troops,
> May taste fate to e'm; Mowe e'm out a passage,
> And, entring where the foremost Squadrons yield,
> Begin the noble Harvest of the Field.
> (1.447b–53)

163

The *noble harvest* makes a moral contrast and a deeper identity with the harvested praise of love in the third act, when Antony has freshly returned from the field.

> There's no satiety of Love in thee:
> Enjoy'd, thou still art new; perpetual Spring
> Is in thy armes; the ripen'd fruit but falls,
> And blossoms rise to fill its empty place;
> And I grow rich by giving.
>
> (3.24–28)

The empty place is rich; the ripened fruit is a perpetual spring; to give is to have. Love has found out a way to live by dying, and in ways which go beyond and over the fruit of this praise. Dolabella's "kindly warmth" (3.190) is almost an immediate response to the word "death" (3.187) after an elaborate praise of Cleopatra. The kindly is nature; the warmth is harvesting; the images impend on death. After Octavia leaves, Cleopatra expresses her faintness by saying "My sight grows dim, and every object dances, / And swims before me, in the maze of death" (3.470–71). Dance, maze, death. She ends a finer speech to Dolabella with a finer ambiguity:

> Could you not beg
> An hour's admittance to his private ear?
> Like one who wanders through long barren Wilds
> And yet foreknows no hospitable Inn
> Is near to succour hunger,
> Eats his fill, before his painful march:
> So would I feed a while my famish'd eyes
> Before we part; for I have far to go,
> If death be far, and never must return.
>
> (4.207–15)

"If death be far" is an idiom for certainty. She is saying that death is surely far, the very stuff of farness, yet also the "if" says "if."

In the fourth act, Antony uses an image of innocence among faithlessness which stirs these notes once more (4.489–93a). Such images grow apace in the last part. An image for love hid in jealousy touches a stranger note of darkness: "Where it lies hid in Shades, watchful in silence" (5.51). Serapion's cry of horror (5.70b–75a) may suggest that time, not only Egypt's day, is closed up.

Antony's melancholy increases into two superb images:

> I will not fight: there's no more work for War.
> The bus'ness of my angry hours is done.
>
> (5.261–62)

> My Torch is out; and the World stands before me
> Like a black Desart, at th' approach of night:
> I'll lay me down, and stray no farther on.
>
> (5.286–88)

Ruth Wallerstein has, in highest praise of lines 286–87, regretted line 288.[20] Yet I think there is need for it, for the metrical resolution, the sense of time straying almost casually on beyond his stopping, the childlikeness of the new sleep.

The death scene of Ventidius and Antony is mostly Roman nobility and friendship but "Thou robbs't me of my death" (5.330a) has a chiller note, a note softened but present in Antony's farewell to Cleopatra.

> But grieve not, while thou stay'st,
> My last disastrous times:

Think we have had a clear and glorious day;
And Heav'n did kindly to delay the storm
Just till our close of ev'ning. Ten years love,
And not a moment lost, but all improv'd
To th'utmost joys: What Ages have we liv'd?
And now to die each other's; and, so dying,
While hand in hand we walk in Groves below,
Whole Troops of Lovers Ghosts shall flock about us,
And all the Train be ours.

(5.387–97)

Then Cleopatra's greatest speech (which owes something to Shakespeare, but so do the themes I speak of)
winds within the varied images—sleep, death, maze,
dream, deceit, love—finally and most quietly into a view
of the rhythm of the whole poem:

Welcom, thou kind Deceiver!
Thou best of Thieves; who, with an easie key,
Dost open life, and, unperceiv'd by us,
Ev'n steal us from our selves: discharging so
Death's dreadful office, better than himself,
Touching our limbs so gently into slumber,
That Death stands by, deceiv'd by his own Image,
And thinks himself but Sleep.

(5.473–80a)

9

A Laurel: The Greatness of Dryden

EVERY SERIOUS STUDY should be its own apology, a self-argument that its energy has been well spent. If one writes about a great poet, one presumes that greatness and attempts to prove it in all one says. The greatness of Dryden should be easy to prove, an eminently visible truth.

He wrote, by any genuine standard, great poems. He wrote not only great satirical poems, but great love poems, great political poems, and great religious poems. Beyond those poems, he wrote many great passages of poetry. He wrote an astonishing amount of good poetry, probably more than any other poet in the language except Shakespeare and Milton. He and Jonson are the masters in English of the middle to high middle styles, and Dryden is the better of the two: he does more in more ways. In Jonson's "To Heaven" and Dryden's "To the Memory of Mr. Oldham" such a style, by its perfecting, becomes profounder than would be otherwise imaginable. Dryden is successful in a wider variety of genres than any other English poet, with the barely possible exception of Chaucer. He is one of the best and funniest comic writers. His satire is noble, not petulant. He is one of the very best metrists, with extraordinary powers of design. He is, beyond shadow of quibble, one of the best English critics, and he may be the best. His critical theory is sound, and his experience as a poet deeply informs its graceful, metaphorical speech, neither abstract formulary nor impressionistic caprice, to which a reader (certainly this reader) always returns with gratitude and delight. He has plausibly been called the father of English criticism. He is the father of much that is best in English prose style.

He has faults (as do all the great poets) and not to be candid about them would be to violate the very spirit of the man, whose candor about himself is one of his most attractive qualities. Throughout this book I have tried to speak plainly about what appeared to me defective in his work. His chief faults as a poet are the following: a too neat view of intrinsic propriety which sometimes cost him the real propriety of the more mixed language of Shakespeare and Milton; energetic, unsuccessful attempts at the sublime; too public handsomenesses of style which go bravura or gaudy; sycophancy which admits mitigation but not entire acquittal; [1] smug Restoration bawdry.

Those faults are overwhelmingly outweighed by his virtues, and are not permeating. His best poems are free (or all but free) of them. *All for Love* has only a very few weak moments. *Absalom and Achitophel* has just one minor flaw of execution.[2] *Anne Killigrew* ranges from the sublime to the impressively competent. *Mac*

Flecknoe is as perfect in sustained development and exact control of tone as poetry ever gets. So in its good-natured way is *Alexander's Feast* and in their separate great ways *To the Memory of Mr. Oldham* and *Veni, Creator Spiritus*. So are the great personal passages in *Religio Laici* and *The Hind and the Panther*, passages which almost constitute separable poems. So is *I feed a flame within*. So are *The Lady's Song*, the Purcell Ode, the translation of Horace's 29th Ode, Third Book, and *Fairest Isle all Isles Excelling*.

The case is plain, then, and must stand. Dryden's is a proven greatness, not truly to be resisted. Enemies are no problem. Dryden could handle them in life, as Shadwell, Milbourne and others flamboyantly well discovered, and since his death he has had few enemies of consequence. Wordsworth is too much like Dryden in nobility and clarity of spirit, and he learned too much from Dryden, to count as an enemy. His poetic apprenticeship was hampered by some habits of diction for which Dryden was partly responsible, and he complained a little.

Friends, however, have done their harm. Arnold's damage is done, and is probably not to be undone, despite the wiser words of some modern scholars. About all one can do is to mutter as frequently and in as wide company as possible, "Poets of our prose indeed!"

There remain T. S. Eliot and Mark Van Doren and Louis Bredvold. There remains, in fact, a general and peculiar attitude towards Dryden in much of the criticism about him, an attitude hard to define and consequently hard to cope with.[3] It is in some measure a question of tones apologetic or condescending. John Dryden needs no apologies. He knew his strength; he could afford his faults; he bore them with ease, with even (as Johnson saw) [4] a smile of some satisfaction.

How can one rationally condescend to the author of *All for Love, Absalom and Achitophel, To the Memory of Mr. Oldham,* the Anne Killigrew ode, the translation of *Veni, Creator Spiritus, Mac Flecknoe, The Lady's Song, An Essay of Dramatic Poesy,* the Preface to *The Fables?* One can, with Hazelton Spencer, in tones of contempt approaching the lewd, look down on him for being inferior to Shakespeare. Is he inferior to Shakespeare? Why, yes. Dryden graciously and beautifully said so. And if Dryden is inferior to Shakespeare, what are we?

As for Eliot and Van Doren (Bredvold is a special but important case I shall not deal with here),[5] the best thing one can say of them is that they are enthusiastic and that they were trying to lift a fallen reputation. But in the process they, with Arnold's prim help, pretty well froze into position the worst mistakes about Dryden.[6]

Eliot tells us in the first paragraph of his essay [7] that "Dryden is one of the tests of a catholic appreciation of poetry," and adds that we "cannot . . . rightly estimate a hundred years of English poetry unless we fully enjoy Dryden." He does say "enjoy," but manages to make Dryden sound incurably special and incurably "period," of historical interest to pedants dusty enough to care. He argues that Dryden's work is not prosaic, but also says that we should admire him for what he made of his material and that Dryden's language states, but fails to suggest. That is, Dryden's material is prosaic, and his style prosaic. He quotes a passage from *The Secular Masque,* a delightful, not fully serious performance, against a fully serious passage from Shelley; and uses

Dryden to support Eliot's early, later repented, deroga-
tion of Milton. He quotes several funny, unsubtle passages (the silly passage from *Aureng-Zebe* isn't even
funny) to give a typical view of Dryden's talents, and
tells us that Dryden's drama is "obviously inferior" to
(all?) Elizabethan and French drama, and that Dryden
had a "commonplace mind." His worst crime against
taste is to apply Van Doren's phrase "like a gong" (used
by Van Doren of the couplets in the heroic plays) to one
of the most delicate and romantic passages in *All for
Love.*

There is more to say than this of Eliot's essay; he
opened eyes to some of Dryden's virtues, and helped to
right a balance. But the overwhelming effect is to put
Dryden in a snugly second-rate position and, despite
Eliot's disclaimers, a prosaic one. He also tends to alien-
ate, deliberately and harmfully, by his contrasts, anyone
who likes Shelley, the romantics in general, or Milton.
He finds, to be sure, something to admire. But Dryden is
not a handsome old-fashioned workhorse; he is a poet.

Van Doren treats Dryden a little better, but in total
impact not much better. His is an admirable and frustrating book. Van Doren is often right, and I find myself
tracking in his snow. The ideal that the book in its first
form, a thesis, represents is wholly admirable and to be
emulated, if they dare, as apparently they dare not, by
other graduate students: an attempt "to say all [one
can] . . . about an important writer, in whatever language seemed suitable," [8] as Van Doren says in his preface to the third edition, which preface itself is one of the
best critical essays on Dryden. Van Doren attempts to
emulate Dryden in the ease of looking at large and talk-

ing in what images come to hand. If the ease slips to glibness, and the style lacks the perfection of Dryden's prose, the book is still a pleasure to read, especially in comparison with the professional and it-would-appear-deliberate atrocities of style committed by many literary scholars.

But charm also has its price, and that price can be, I fear, truth. Take the ending of Van Doren's book: assured, neatly balanced, and highly quotable. But, finally, a heavy disservice to the great writer he is attempting to be, in his interestingly wry phrase, "more or less enthusiastic"[9] about:

> If there was something fatuous about the opulence of the Augustans there is often something desperate about the simplicity of the moderns. If an aristocratic society fattens and sleeks the poets of its choice, democracy grinds many of its sons to powder. A man who composes verse too exclusively out of his faculties can hardly be judged by men who write too much with their nerves; the imagination, the umpire of art, might acknowledge neither. Dryden lives not as one who went out to rear great frames of thought and feeling, nor as one who waited within himself and caught fine, fugitive details of sensation, but as one who elastically paced the limits of a dry and well-packed mind. He braces those who listen to his music; he will be found refreshing if, answering his own invitation,
>
> > When tired with following nature, you think fit,
> > To seek repose in the cool shades of wit.

It sounds like good polemics; but I am not sure that it is even that. Does it really persuade against moderns? Does

172

it really mean to? Its actual persuading is that Dryden is a second-rate sort of poet. It says or hints that his poetry is fatuous, fat and sleek, unimaginative, over and coldly rhetorical, incapable of great design or fine feelings. Dryden is, in an almost inexplicably damnatory metaphor, the elastic pacer of a well-packed mind; he is, though, very pleasant in a minor league sort of way if one isn't much interested in "following nature." The very loveliness of Dryden's couplet is used to exclude him from the kingdom of nature and high imagination.

Remarks which presume and engrave the romantic assumptions about Dryden run throughout the book, frequently supported by quotation of Dryden's very worst lines.[10] The book comes uncomfortably close to turning Dryden into pure Doeg who "Faggotted his Notions as they fell, / And if they Rhim'd and Rattl'd all was well." Energy, bounce, bright, impetuosity, statement [11]—words like that Van Doren has in plenty, and as many denials of finer things.

The objection is simple enough: Van Doren is wrong. One could damage any great poet by the same methods. The sort of impression one could create, by faggoting their horrors, of Chaucer, Shakespeare, Donne, Shelley, Keats, would shudder a marrowbone. Good poets write much bad poetry.

No great frames of thought and feeling? *Anne Killigrew, Absalom and Achitophel, All for Love,* are not?

No fine and fugitive details of feeling? No imagination? No romantic fancy? This book abounds in examples. One may add these.[12]

> We wander in the fields of air below,
> Changelings and fools of heaven . . .

And music dying in remoter sounds

Musick unbought, that minister'd Delight
To Morning-walks, and lull'd his Cares by Night:

But when the tedious Twilight wears away,
And Stars grow paler at th' approach of Day

Miriads of blewest Plagues lye underneath 'em,
And more than Aconite has dipt the Silk.

God's Image, God's Anointed lay
    Without Motion, Pulse or Breath,
A Senseless Lump of Sacred Clay,
    An Image, now, of Death.

But when he spoke, what tender words he said!
So softly, that, like flakes of feathered snow,
They melted as they fell.

Deep into some thick covert would I run,
Impenetrable to the stars or sun,
And fenced from day, by night's eternal skreen;
Unknown to heaven, and to myself unseen.

These are enow for me, in faith enow.
Their bodies shall not flag while I can lead;
Nor wearied limbs confess mortality,
Before those ants, that blacken all yon hill,
Are crept into the earth. Farewell.

O Daughter of the Rose, whose Cheeks unite
The diff'ring Titles of the Red and White

or, more familiar:

A milk white *Hind,* immortal and unchang'd,
Fed on the lawns, and in the forest rang'd;
Without unspotted, innocent within,
She fear'd no danger, for she knew no sin.

174

Thy generous fruits, though gather'd ere their prime
Still shew'd a quickness; and maturing time
But mellows what we write to the dull sweets of
Rime.

And streight, with in-born Vigour, on the Wing,
Like mounting Larkes, to the New Morning sing.

That's a baker's dozen. There are many more. Not count-
ing the fine and fugitive shades of feelings and high,
various imagination in other sorts of poetic effect even
more typically Dryden's.

For those tired of following nature? That is surely the
root and ultimate insult to a critic and poet who made
the "great foundation" of nature the ground and fabric
of his literary existence.

His poetic assumptions stand in nature, the created,
vital, various, ordered world which includes natural
(moral and esthetic) law. Nature is the subject of imitation; the foundation of the natural accords between
world, poet, work of art, and audience that make poetry
and criticism possible; and the standard for judgment.
The primary subject of poetry is human nature (conceived as an integral part of greater nature) and, within
human nature, action and passions. The passions are
deep, various, responsive to the permanent forms of
experience and to the moral law. The end of poems is
delight, but only just images of nature can produce delight. The spirit of man cannot be satisfied but with
truth and justice, because his deepest urge is for reality,
and reality (nature) is at once true and moral.

Such a poetics is absolutist in fundamentals and Dryden makes it intelligently flexible in practice. Its abso-
lutism avoids the arbitrary because it is founded on

permanent human nature; experience has its rights, and the *consensus gentium* speaks with a real, though not an infallible, authority. More ultimately, such standards are not arbitrary because the natural world is created and natural law is rooted in the divine. Human nature is more than just what men have happened to be; men can succumb to the unnatural in art or morals and do violence to their human nature (and a million who are evil represent permanent human nature less well than one man who fills the frame) and therefore do violence to the vital order in which human nature has its proper place. Dryden keeps a balance between experience and the ideal. His theory allows for the balance. Sometimes as a critic he insists that what truly delights must, even though it goes against accepted rules, be in some real accord with nature. When he so argues, he may sound preromantic. On the other hand, he sometimes argues that the rules are based on observation of nature, and that art based on them is necessarily sound (and must, by implication, delight a good judge). When he does, he may sound like a pedant contemptuous of experience. Yet his theory provides for both emphases: what pleases a good judge must be sound; what is sound must please a good judge. He feels some rules are certain (for example, that art must imitate nature, and must be just and lively); but holds that the secondary rules admit but probable reasoning. Hence he allows for experience, tradition, reason, rules, inspiration, taste.

His theory is flexible in another, highly important way. His basic theory is that art imitates; yet he was too good a poet not to have a feeling for the rights of the work of art in itself. That feeling is shown in the word "image" (an image is an object with its own form as well as an imitation) in his famous phrase "just and lively image of nature," in the double sense of the "proper" in diction or imagery (proper in itself, and proper to subject), and in the emphasis on harmony (intrinsically pleasing sound) as well as propriety (appropriateness to subject) in his theory of versification. His respect for form is likewise shown in the many prose metaphors through which he allows both for theory and for the densities of the actual experience of the practicing poet.

His notion of propriety is also strongly at work in his poetry. His diction is pure, uneccentric, sometimes luminous. His notion of propriety as a good in itself and his feeling for the sharp distinctions of the genres cost him some of the power and real propriety of diction achieved by some other great poets. Even so, his diction is capable of great splendor. His imagery is governed by his sense of propriety and his feeling for clear analogies between man and physical nature; his images are normally sharply defined, clearly appropriate, with little fusion of vehicle and tenor. He failed to see how far language is metaphorical; hence he misses effects that the metaphysicals and the romantics, in their different ways, gain. But his best imagery is distinguished by power, versatility, and beauty; when he is true to himself, he, unlike the metaphysicals, is not tempted to contorted (and heartless) ingenuity; unlike the romantics, he almost never confuses or blurs his images.

That the images Dryden prefers verge on the trite is no accident. When Dryden is trite, he is splendid; [13] his mind takes fire with great commonplaces, in which general qualities apply widely and deeply to the most serious human affairs, in which a large view of the world receives literary sanction. To miss the clarity and (in Johnson's phrase) "the grandeur of generality" is to miss much of the best in Dryden. But, a good emulator, he applies his commonplaces with originality; not an originality that refutes what good men have long known but that reinforces and extends truth by exactness of application. He ranges the world for images that light up the mind, images from a physical world he much loved (he loved the country, he loved fishing), yet would order in response to value. For value is, in the deepest possible sense, natural too. Dryden followed nature.

How great a poet is Dryden? Too great for us to patronize, is my immediate if surly reply. Great enough for our gratitude. Greater than even his more sympathetic critics of the late nineteenth and the twentieth century have felt; that I believe. After Shakespeare and Milton? Yes. After Chaucer? Well, yes. After that, one just might do some quarreling. Not to rank him above any of the other poets who deserve our high love and admiration; just to number him with his peers. Dryden can dine at journey's end not only with Donne (and Yeats), but with Wordsworth and Shelley and rare Ben and great Spenser and their other (few) companions. And, if it is a question of ranking men of letters, his position has to be high among peers.

Virtually no one would deny that he is one of the half dozen of the best English critics, that as a critic he ranks with Coleridge and Johnson and Arnold and Pope and perhaps another or so. One could make an interestingly stout case that he is the best English critic. Not the greatest; Coleridge and Johnson are greater; but, it may be, the best.[14] Coleridge is profounder, more fascinating, more seminal, more the professional of ideas, but

178

he is also far more spotty, more uneven of style, and more disorganized. By being more the philosopher he is just somewhat less the true critic. Johnson has more range and more authority; his logic and his rhetoric are more commanding; he also has more blind spots, and more stiffness of style and judgment. His love of wit and his love of victory in argument cost him qualification and consistency; Dryden's spirit is suppler and sweeter: it helps him tell truth. Shelley and Wordsworth and Pope wrote less. Arnold has more crucial vaguenesses, and more tics of style. I'm not really persuaded that Dryden is the best critic; I don't think it absurd to say that he may be.

His criticism has certainly never lacked praise. Yet in recent years it has been too often praised for its minor virtues, too little admired for its major ones. One reads often that Dryden's criticism is sprightly, tentative, conversational and urbane in tone. One less often hears that it is wise, true, and firmly founded. Yet it is a criticism great in content as well as in style. Its very urbanity and freedom are possible only because of Dryden's certainty about its foundation. The fundamental rules are absolute; the secondary rules admit probable reasoning. The combination makes for a balance that Dryden's practice keeps. Dryden's ontological faith, his basic trust in the reality and order of nature, is of great service to him there. His confidence saves him from the necessity of continually probing his root convictions and thereby permits him the free use of his basic principles; at the same time the certain foundation saves his criticism, for all its variety of approach and perception, for all its gentlemanly elegances and its succumbings to occasions, from mere eclecticism or the quicksands of relativism. Further, his sense of propriety rooted in nature and his related sense of the clear, natural accords between work, audience, and subject permit the lucidity and precision of his thought and style. There is no clearer, better balanced, or more inclusive criticism in English.

As a poet he possesses, in no trivial measure, those very qualities which are denied him: depth, psychological insight, subtlety, romantic delicacy, and strangeness. The dark of the moon is not his region; but he forages there. And he possesses in huge and rewarding abundance those virtues he is allowed to have. They are major virtues.

Of politics, one should say little or a complicated much. In this book, I have chosen to say little. I disagree with some of his doctrines, but I respect them. I believe that his views have been often misunderstood, and that there are important things to learn from him about the grounds of legitimacy, the relation of freedom to order, the dangers of tyranny hidden within some vigorously egalitarian noises, noises which are growing louder as I write.

I am convinced of (1) the essential solidity and sincerity of his Christian faith throughout his adult life, an untimid and, despite Bredvold, not merely a sceptical-conservative-fideistic faith, (2) the increasing dignity, sweetness, and courage of his piety after he became a Catholic. When one sums up the evidence, which is poems and passages of poems, I think one has to say that Dryden is a great religious poet. That may be a startling claim. All I say in its defense is, listen to the evidence.

180

His personality grows on one. I see no reason to disagree with Congreve.[15] Dryden was a courteous, thoughtful, friendly, candid, shy yet charming man, and the very paucity of what his determined, and highly motivated, enemies could gather against his moral character is dramatic evidence for his essential personal decency.

The final evidence for the merit of a poet is the poems. If that evidence will not convince, conviction is not to be had. The best political poem in the language. The best lampoon in the language, *Mac Flecknoe,* one so good that it raises the genre of lampoon to a metaphysical dignity of satire. Another of the best lampoons in the language, *The Medal.* One of the best English Pindaric Odes, *To the Pious Memory of Mistress Anne Killigrew.* Other excellent odes. The best verse play in the last three hundred years, *All for Love.* One of the finest personal elegies in any language, *To the Memory of Mr. Oldham.* In the verse essay, an important genre, rivaled only by Pope. In a delightful genre, the prologue-epilogue, totally without a rival. Some of the best and most original English translations. Some very fine songs, and some other admirably skillful ones of lesser substance. And more.

Dryden's poetry is often seen as craftsmanlike, rich in purely metrical energy, formally proper to genre. So indeed it is. But it is far more: it is, throughout its whole range, alive with a special kind of feeling, a really metaphysical excitement. Even his urbanity is luminous. To achieve formal excellence is, so Dryden thought and deeply felt, justly to image a vital and luminous nature that worked in man, the genres, the moral law, the rules of art. Such feeling accompanies, surrounds, and strengthens the many and various feelings responsive to the heights and depths of man's nature and the world. One can justly call it an ontological poetry. And that, by Dryden's own, and true, standards, is enough of a compliment.

Key to Scansion

i	iamb
I	strong iamb (iamb with a fairly strong unstressed syllable)
i	weak iamb (iamb with a fairly weak stressed syllable)
t *	trochee
a	anapest
a₁	anapest with a fairly strong first unstressed syllable
a₂	anapest with a fairly strong second unstressed syllable
a₁.₂	anapest with a fairly strong first and second unstressed syllable
d *	dactyl
p	pyrrhic
s	spondee
b	amphibrach
x	truncated foot
<	feminine ending
|	pause, phrase-end, or caesura

* Capitals and italics are used to show special effects with trochees as with iambs to indicate variations in stress; subscripts similarly with dactyls. Any iamb may be marked i; similarly with other feet.

Notes

The first eight chapter titles, in order, were taken from the following works by Dryden: Heroic Stanzas on Cromwell, v. 96; Preface to *Annus Mirabilis* (Watson, I, *100*); Song I from *The Conquest of Granada*, v. 1; *Annus Mirabilis*, v. 572; *Absalom and Achitophel*, v. 838; *Absalom and Achitophel*, v. 935; *Veni, Creator Spiritus*, v. 18; *All for Love*, 3.471.

1

[1] John Dryden, "A Discourse Concerning the Original and Progress of Satire," *Of Dramatic Poesy and Other Critical Essays*, ed. George Watson, 2 vols. (New York, 1962), II, *73–74*. This edition is hereafter called Watson. See also *Essays of John Dryden*, ed. W. P. Ker, 2 vols. (New York, 1961), II, *17*. This edition is hereafter called Ker.

[2] Dedication of *The Rival Ladies*, Watson, I, *3–4* (Ker, I, *3*).

[3] The phrase "a pretty thinly diluted ideal of order" is applied to Dryden's age by Douglas Bush in *English Literature in the Earlier Seventeenth Century:1600–1660*, 2d ed. (Oxford, 1962), *422*. On page *419* he says flatly, "Milton was a poet; Dryden a man of letters." On pages *423–24* he admits, cheerfully if tardily, that his view of the Augustans is unfair, "exaggerated" and "foreshortened." Cp. Ruth Wallerstein, "Dryden and the Analysis of Shakespeare's Techniques," *Essential Articles for the Study of John Dryden*, ed. H. T. Swedenberg, Jr. (Hamden, Conn., 1966), *573*, (the book is hereafter called *Articles*) who speaks of his "vulgar spirit . . . in many areas" and his "spiritually shallow milieu" and in another essay of "the thin spiritual air he often had to breathe" ("On the Death of Mrs. Killigrew," *Articles, 584*). Of course that in a way is true, as it is true for all poets and all people. Even granting some particularly unpleasant features to his milieu, features which Dryden was finally roundly to criticize, there remains a sort of trick of association we are apt to play, thinking of Dryden at the theater or the coffeehouses rather than in the woods, or at church—or in his study. Earl Miner has an

interesting phrase (among many others in his book) in a note on Herschel Baker's *Wars of Truth:* he says that Baker makes the "usual mistake" of "assuming the death by midcentury of ideas, assumptions and beliefs very much alive in Dryden." *Dryden's Poetry* (Bloomington, Ind., 1967), *340*, note 31.

⁴ As is held by Mark Van Doren, *John Dryden*, 3rd ed. (New York, 1946), *53–56*.

⁵ As is held by J. E. Spingarn, ed., *Critical Essays of the Seventeenth Century*, 3 vols. (Bloomington, Ind., 1957), I, *lxvii–lxviii*.

⁶ As is held by A. O. Lovejoy, "The Parallel of Deism and Classicism," *Essays in the History of Ideas* (Baltimore, Md., 1948), *79–82, 89–95*.

⁷ As is unfortunately (and in Lovejoy's instance deliberately) suggested by the useful compilatory studies, Lovejoy, " 'Nature' as Aesthetic Norm," *Essays Ideas, 69–77;* A. O. Lovejoy and George Boas, *Primitivism and Related Ideas in Antiquity* (Baltimore, Md., 1935), *447–56;* Harold S. Wilson, "Some Meanings of 'Nature' in Renaissance Literary Theory," *Journal of the History of Ideas*, II (October 1941), *430–48*. Cp. Clarence C. Green, *The Neo-Classic Theory of Tragedy* . . . (New York, 1966), *69:* "Nature meant whatever you wanted it to mean." It did not.

⁸ "A Defence of an Essay of Dramatic Poesy," Watson, I, *122* (Ker, I, *123*).

⁹ "An Essay of Dramatic Poesy," Watson, I, *25* (Ker, I, *36*).

¹⁰ "Dramatic Poesy," Watson, I, *47* (Ker, I, *59*).

¹¹ "Defence of an Essay," Watson, I, *122* (Ker, I, *123*). See Hoyt Trowbridge, "The Place of Rules in Dryden's Criticism," *Modern Philology*, XLIV (November 1946), *84–96* (*Articles, 112–34*). Trowbridge's views are endorsed by W. K. Wimsatt, Jr. and Cleanth Brooks, *Literary Criticism* (New York, 1957), *192–93* and note on *193*. Trowbridge's essay, since it points the most essential distinction, is in my judgment the most important single essay on Dryden's criticism, even though Trowbridge's insistence on the "rational" in discussing Dryden's rational probabilism makes him seriously underplay the importance of taste (perception, response) in Dryden's dialectic. Frank Huntley, *On Dryden's "Essay of Dramatic Poesy"* (Ann Arbor, Mich., 1951), argues that Dryden maintains consistency through a dialectic of shifting emphases on *inventio, dispositio, elocutio*. Ronald S. Crane, "English Neoclassical Criticism," *Critics and Criticism*, ed. Ronald S. Crane (Chicago, 1952), *376*, explains apparent neoclassical inconsistency in terms of a dialectic involving art, artist, work, and

audience. Both sets of terms are important in Dryden's criticism; Crane's set is more inclusive than Huntley's; neither set is so inclusive or central as these two essays tend to suggest. Dryden's dialectic ranges.

[12] See, among others, George Saintsbury, *A History of Criticism . . .* , 3 vols. (London, 1900–1904), II (1902); J. E. Spingarn, *A History of Literary Criticism in the Renaissance,* 2d ed. (New York, 1908); Benedetto Croce, *Aesthetic,* trans. Douglass Ainslie, 2d ed. (New York, 1922), esp. *189–203;* René Bray, *La Formation de la Doctrine Classique en France* (Paris, 1931); Katharine Everett Gilbert and Helmut Kuhn, *A History of Esthetics* (New York, 1939), esp. *162–232;* John W. H. Atkins, *English Literary Criticism: 17th and 18th Centuries* (London, 1951); Crane, "Neoclassical," *Critics, 372–88;* Wimsatt and Brooks, *Criticism, 174–251;* Alexander W. Allison, *Toward an Augustan Poetic* (Lexington, Ky., 1962); O. B. Hardison, *The Enduring Monument* (Chapel Hill, 1962); Paul Ramsey, *The Lively and the Just* (Tuscaloosa, Ala., 1962), *1–40, 131–42;* K. G. Hamilton, *The Two Harmonies* (Oxford, 1963); "Neoclassical Poetics," *Encyclopedia of Poetry and Poetics* (Princeton, 1965), *559–64; Studies in Criticism and Aesthetics 1660–1800: Studies in Honor of Samuel Holt Monk,* ed. Howard P. Anderson and John S. Shea (Minneapolis, 1967); James William Johnson, *The Formation of English Neo-Classical Thought* (Princeton, 1967).

[13] Cp. Miner, *Dryden's Poetry:* "Without his critical force of comparison, Dryden would not have become our first great literary critic" (*83*).

[14] Preface to *Sylvae,* Watson, II, *29* (Ker, I, *264*).

[15] Preface to *Troilus and Cressida,* Watson, I, *247* (Ker, I, *212*).

[16] 1668 Prologue to *Secret Love, or the Maiden Queen,* vv. 8–9. This quotation, and all other quotations from Dryden's poems, are, unless otherwise stated, from *The Poems of John Dryden,* ed. James Kinsley, 4 vols. (Oxford, 1957).

[17] "Dramatic Poesy," Watson, I, *61* (Ker, I, *73*).

[18] "Dramatic Poesy," Watson, I, *59* (Ker, I, *70–71*); and *Sylvae,* Watson, II, *32–33* (Ker, I, *268*). The word "naturally" is in Watson, I, *59.*

[19] Preface to *Annus Mirabilis,* Watson, I, *99* (Ker, I, *16*).

[20] "Author's Apology," Watson, I, *207* (Ker, I, *190*). Cp. Dedication of *The Spanish Friar,* Watson, I, *278* (Ker, I, *248*); *Sylvae,* Watson, II, *22* (Ker, I, *256*); Preface to *Albion and Albanius,*

Watson, II, *34* (Ker, I, *270*); "The Life of Lucian," Watson, II, *210–11* (not in Ker).

[21] "Author's Apology," Watson, I, *200–201* (Ker, I, *183*); "A Parallel Betwixt Painting and Poetry," Watson, II, *201* (Ker, II, *145*).

[22] "Author's Apology," Watson, I, *203* (Ker, I, *186*).

[23] That tradition, rooted in the classical rhetoricians, is discussed in relation to Dryden in Lillian Feder's "John Dryden's Interpretation and Use of Latin Poetry," unpublished Ph.D. dissertation (University of Minnesota, 1951), *47–66;* Huntley, *On Dryden's "Essay of Dramatic Poesy," 13–17;* and Samuel Holt Monk's review of Huntley's monograph in *Philological Quarterly,* XXXI (July 1952), *269–70.*

[24] See, for style, Preface to *Mirabilis,* Watson, I, *100–101* (Ker, I, *17–18*), *Sylvae,* Watson, II, *20* (Ker, I, *253–54*); Preface to *Eleonora,* Watson, II, *61* (not in Ker); for imagery, "Author's Apology," Watson, I, *205* (Ker, I, *188*); for steps of the making, Preface to the *Fables,* Watson, II, *275–76* (Ker, II, *252–53*). Some such simplification is inherent in the process of talking about poetry, but there are better and worse degrees.

[25] An idea I argue at more length in *Lively, 17–29, 99–135.*

[26] "A Discourse Concerning Satire," Watson, II, *144–45* (Ker, II, 102).

[27] "Defence of an Essay," Watson, I, *120* (Ker, I, *121*) (emphasis Dryden's).

[28] Watson, I, *59* (Ker, I, *70–71*), correcting "state" by Ker's "stage." Cp. "Satire," Watson, II, *145* (Ker, II, *103*).

[29] "Dramatic Poesy," Watson, I, *91* (Ker, I, *107*).

[30] *Sylvae,* Watson, II, *20–21* (Ker, I, *253–54*).

[31] *Mirabilis,* ("apt") Watson, I, *98* (Ker, I, *15*); "Albion," Watson, II, *40* (Ker, I, *277*).

[32] Cp. D. T. Mace, "Musical Humanism, the Doctrine of Rhythmus, and the Saint Cecilia Odes of Dryden," *Journal of the Warburg and Courtauld Institutes,* XXVII (1964), *280–81.*

[33] John Crowe Ransom, *The New Criticism* (Norfolk, Conn., 1941), *294–300,* cuts the knot by denying any connection. See Yvor Winters' comments on Ransom's position in *In Defense of Reason* (London, 1960), *342–52.*

[34] Dedication of the *Aeneid,* Watson, II, *236–37* (Ker, II, *217*).

[35] R. D. Jameson, "Notes on Dryden's Lost Prosodia," *Modern Philology,* XX (February 1923), *241–53.*

[36] See D. T. Mace, "The Doctrine of Sound and Sense in Augus-

tan Poetic Theory," *Review of English Studies,* new series, II (April 1951), *129–39.*

[37] Watson, II, *32.* "Numbers" means technically the varying number of feet in Pindaric lines, but not merely that.

[38] The Latin means "what I am unable to say, and what I feel so much."

[39] Miner, *Dryden's Poetry, 249,* speaks of "the real grace of cadence beneath the appearance of roughness" in this line.

[40] Cp. George McFadden's excellent essay, "Dryden and the Numbers of His Native Tongue," *Essays and Studies in Language and Literature,* ed. Herbert H. Petit (Pittsburgh, 1964), *87–109,* esp. *91.*

2

[1] R. D. Jameson, "Notes on Dryden's Lost Prosodia," *Modern Philology* XX (February 1923), *241;* George R. Stewart, *The Technique of English Verse* (New York, 1930), *182–89;* Robert L. Sharp, *From Donne to Dryden* (Chapel Hill, 1940), *173–75;* Mark Van Doren, *John Dryden,* 3rd ed. (New York, 1946), *56–66.* There are valuable remarks on sound-sense relations (and all such remarks support the idea of imitative harmony) in Arthur W. Verrall, *Lectures on Dryden,* ed. Margaret de G. Verrall (New York, 1964), *194–99;* René Wellek and Austin Warren, *Theory of Literature,* 3rd ed. (New York, 1962), *158–73;* Yvor Winters, *In Defense of Reason* (London, 1960), *542–52;* W. K. Wimsatt, Jr., *The Verbal Icon* (Lexington, Ky., 1954), *152–66,* esp. *165–66;* George Hemphill, ed., *Discussions of Poetry: Rhythm and Sound* (Boston, 1961), esp. the essays by Chatman and Stein; John Thompson, Jr., *The Founding of English Metre* (London, 1961), *1–14, 156;* Harvey Gross, *Sound and Form in Modern Poetry* (Ann Arbor, Mich., 1964), *10–23;* George McFadden, "Dryden and the Numbers of His Native Tongue," *Essays and Studies in Language and Literature,* ed. Herbert H. Petit (Pittsburgh, 1964), *87–109;* W. K. Wimsatt, Jr. and Monroe C. Beardsley, "The Concept of Meter," *Hateful Contraries* (Lexington, Ky., 1965), *108–45.*

[2] Van Doren, viii.

[3] *Ibid., 63* (emphasis his).

[4] Samuel Johnson, "Alexander Pope," *Lives of the English Poets,* ed. G. B. Hill, 3 vols. (Oxford, 1905), III, *231* (emphasis his).

[5] Johnson, "Samuel Butler," *Lives,* I, *217.*

[6] Van Doren, *66.*

[7] Emphasis mine in all four examples.

3

[1] In which he was unique in his time, according to Catharine Peltz, "The Neo-Classic Lyric 1660–1725," *ELH,* XI (June 1944), *110.* Cp. Cyrus L. Day, in the introduction to his edition of Dryden's songs, *The Songs of John Dryden* (Cambridge, Mass., 1932), *xi–xii.*

[2] I shall not treat, as outside my competence, their value in relation to their musical settings. They do also exist as poems (see chapter 7, note 9).

[3] Earl Miner, *Dryden's Poetry* (Bloomington, Ind., 1967), says of such songs that "the closer an affair comes to its sexual climax the more lilting the measure is apt to be" (*233*).

[4] "A Discourse Concerning Satire," Watson, II, *76* (Ker, II, *19*).

[5] George Saintsbury, *A History of English Prosody* . . . , 3 vols. (London, 1906–1910), II, *364–65* and note.

[6] See "Key to Scansion."

[7] Dryden uses the same measure for incantation by making the rhythm even slower and more pronounced. See, in *Songs of Dryden,* part of the incantation from act III of *The Indian Queen* (3), dialogue from *The Tempest,* act II (first stanza) (*11–12*), and the incantation from act III of *Oedipus* (*51–52*).

[8] Saintsbury, *History of Prosody,* II, *372–73.*

[9] Since feet are conveniences which do not represent sound units, such a pattern can also be described with equal accuracy, but less economy, as t i a a < ("After the pangs of a desperate Lover"). George McFadden, "Dryden and the Numbers of His Native Tongue," *Essays and Studies in Language and Literature,* ed. Herbert H. Petit (Pittsburgh, 1964), *100–101,* in his metrical analysis, ignores the difference between odd and even lines and describes the patterns as either i i a a or x a a a. Either is accurate for some even lines, but his description ignores the interlacing of the possibilities which gives the effect I attempt to describe.

[10] Or, if "we" gets a sexy tilt, the line may even become five iambs, since the first foot is ambiguous (could be an iamb or a trochee).

¹¹ I use the term "caesura" for a pause that has a definite place in a measure as part of the metrical norm.

¹² A real spondee in English is rare, since our habits of speech are such that of any two successive stresses within a phrase we give one slightly more force than the other. Real spondees can and do occur when the two successive syllables are separated by a pause since in that situation the two syllables can receive equal degrees of stress. Near spondees (two heavy but not equal stresses) are common, especially following two light stresses (near pyrrhic). Real pyrrhics do occur in phrases in which two light successive stresses are indistinguishably weak; near pyrrhics are more common. To call near pyrrhics and near spondees pyrrhics and spondees is useful and only slightly inaccurate, and I shall do so from time to time.

Some metrists are fond of the argument that theoretically pyrrhics and spondees are impossible, since the principle of relative stress applies and of two syllables in succession one must always be, however slightly, more stressed than the other. The argument oddly mixes ideal and actual: in a world in which our ears were so perfect that they could detect even an infinitesimal difference in stress, our vocal organs could with the same ideality make stresses exactly equal.

¹³ Yvor Winters, *In Defense of Reason* (London, 1960), *135–36;* Saintsbury, *History of Prosody,* II, *373;* Miner, *Dryden's Poetry, 238–40.* Miner speaks of the "verse tension" (*239*), but apparently refers mostly to the difference in tone between the anxious first stanza and the joyful second stanza, though he does speak once of the "disturbing, throbbing cadence" (*240*).

¹⁴ Winters, *Defense, 136.*

¹⁵ A term vague (broadly generic) even as critical terms go. Any two connected items are "associated." If *p* entails *q, p* and *q* are associated. If event A causes event B, the events are associated. The term comes to mean loosely or indirectly associated rather than associated through normal structural means.

¹⁶ So is the lovely "Fairest Isle all Isles Excelling," from *King Arthur,* a poem that follows a pleasant metrical base (t t t t in odd lines, t t t x in even) without a single substitution.

4

¹ Preface to *Annus Mirabilis,* Watson, I, *95* (Ker, I, *11–12*).

² Alfred Ainger, in the manuscript (in the Folger Shakespeare

Library) for his Lectures on Dryden, says that the stanza should be called "the *meditative* or *philosophical* stanza" more properly than the "heroic stanza" (emphases his, 7). For discussions of the effect of the form see *The Works of John Dryden*, ed. Sir Walter Scott, 18 vols. (London, 1808), IX, *83–84;* Arthur W. Verrall, *Lectures on Dryden*, ed. Margaret de G. Verrall (New York, 1964), *92–93;* Mark Van Doren, *John Dryden*, 3rd ed. (New York, 1946), *82–84;* Edward N. Hooker, "The Purpose of Dryden's Annus Mirabilis," *Studies in . . . Honor of Arthur Ellicott Case*, ed. Richard C. Boys (Ann Arbor, Mich., 1952), *120–39 (Articles, 281–99); The Works of John Dryden*, ed. Edward N. Hooker and H. T. Swedenberg, Jr., I (Berkeley and Los Angeles, 1956), *193–95; 267–69.* This edition is hereafter referred to as Dryden (Calif.). C. M. Lewis has a very good discussion of the basic effects of stanza forms in *The Principles of English Verse* (New Haven, Conn., 1929), 72–79.

³ A beautiful modern example, Karl Shapiro's "The Sickness of Adam," the first section of his *Adam and Eve*, tells part of a story, of Edenic history, but hesitatingly, strangely, in trancelike and varied rhythms, and with much brooding meditation.

⁴ Quotations from *Heroique Stanzas to . . . Cromwell* and *Annus Mirabilis* are from Dryden (Calif.).

⁵ Dryden (Scott), IX, *3–5;* Kenneth Young, *John Dryden* (London, 1954), *21–27;* Charles E. Ward, *The Life of John Dryden* (Chapel Hill, 1961), *18–19;* Dryden (Calif.), I, *189–91.* One, however, grants some power to the arguments; and the chaos of rapidly changing administrations after Cromwell was no small argument for a new stability.

⁶ Dryden (Scott), IX, *4;* Dryden (Calif.), I, *190–91.*

⁷ The California editors discuss this feature of the heroic quatrain as a means of increasing "strength and stateliness," Dryden (Calif.), I, *268.*

⁸ See Dryden (Calif.) I, *194–95,* whose editors discuss the impact of "warre" against "trade," but not the rhetorical accent.

⁹ Thomas Babington Macaulay, "John Dryden" (1828), *Critical and Historical Essays*, 3 vols. (Boston, 1900), I, *215.*

¹⁰ Bragged on in his preface (Watson, I, *100–102* [Ker, I, *17–19*]) and by pointing out allusions with notes to the poem.

¹¹ See Dryden (Calif.), I, *260–67.*

¹² For one, John Manifold's gay, stirring poem *The Tomb of Lieutenant John Learmonth, A. I. F.*, anthologized in *The War Poets*, ed. Oscar Williams (New York, 1945), *195–96.*

¹³ See Dryden (Calif.), note to verse 38.

[14] As Robert Lowell's *The Quaker Graveyard in Nantucket* (verse 3 of section III) and Homer tell us. Why does Lowell interpret Homer's *kuanochāita* (*Iliad* 13.563 and elsewhere) as blue-haired rather than dark-haired? He has looked at the sea.

[15] Miner, *Dryden's Poetry*, 17.

[16] Dryden (Calif.), note to lines *241–44*.

[17] Miner, *Dryden's Poetry*, referring to a different passage of the poem, on the "almost surrealistic vitality" of "our moments of great suffering" (*12*).

[18] *The Poems of Gray and Collins*, ed. Austin Lane Poole, 3rd ed. (Oxford, 1937), 95.

[19] Miner, *Dryden's Poetry*, discusses this passage, showing truly that Dryden absorbed "the excitement of the new science" (*30*) into his own beliefs, which are Christian and orthodox. Miner says that the meaning of the line "Since best to praise his works is best to know" verse 660 is "Praising a transcendent God for his works is the best *knowledge* man can show" (emphasis Miner's, *29*). Miner denies that Dryden intended the opposite meaning (that scientific knowledge of nature is high praise of God—that is, that "best to know" is the subject of the clause), which meaning would be Deistic. Dryden was, as *Religio Laici* later makes manifest, no Deist; but the grammar and meter of the stanza, the paralleling power of "best" and the authority of "Since" are strong evidence that the meaning Miner rejects is the primary meaning, though both are intended. That meaning is not in itself Deistic or otherwise heretical; it would become so only if made exclusive or idolatrous, which Dryden does not allow. The interpretation of that beautiful line is, however, the minor point. On the major point Miner and I agree: that Dryden's view of science in these lines is Christian and profound. It could, I suppose, be argued that the lines are not very profound since they come to a double tautology: Science knows (something of) what God knows—that is, knowledge knows (something of) what the All-knowing knows. But the lines say more than that, and even the tautology has its profundity. Science *can* know because God wills a partially intelligible world, which he knows and superintends. In Dryden's view, science *should* be used for man's weal rather than his woe, because *should*'s are of the stuff of God's knowledge too. Nature is knowable and includes value, because created. Once more we come to the center of Dryden's convictions.

[20] Some examples are the Prologue to *Aureng-Zebe*, v. 10 (the most familiar); the literally enchanted grounds or groves in

Oedipus, act III, scene 1 (Dryden [Scott], VI, *171–72*); *King Arthur,* act III, scene 1 (Dryden [Scott], VIII, *147*); and *Tyrannic Love,* act I, scene 1 (Dryden [Scott], III, *360*). Others include Dryden (Scott), IV, *161* (*The Conquest of Granada,* part two, act III, scene 1); Dryden (Scott), V, *129* (*The State of Innocence,* act II, scene 1); Dryden (Scott), VIII, *257* (*Cleomenes,* act I, scene 1); Dryden (Scott), VIII, *368* (*Love Triumphant,* act II, scene 1); *The Hind and the Panther,* part III, v. 722; and *The Flower and the Leaf,* v. 149.

[21] A comparable view of providence expressed with comparable beauty appears in Herbert Butterfield, *Christianity and History* (London, 1957), *145–47*.

5

[1] See George Saintsbury, *Historical Manual of English Prosody* (London, 1910), *84–86;* Jakob Schipper, *A History of English Versification* (Oxford, 1910), *217–18;* Robert L. Sharp, *From Donne to Dryden* (Chapel Hill, 1940), *172–74;* Mark Van Doren, *John Dryden,* 3rd ed. (New York, 1946), *59–61, 68–72, 86–87.* See also these articles: Ruth C. Wallerstein, "The Development of the . . . Heroic Couplet . . . ," *PMLA,* L (March 1935), *166–209;* George Williamson, "The Rhetorical Pattern of Neo-Classical Wit," *Modern Philology,* XXXIII (August 1935), *55–81;* George Hemphill, "Dryden's Heroic Line," *PMLA,* LXXII (December 1957), *863–79* (*Articles, 519–40*); McD. Emslie, "Dryden's Couplets," *Essays in Criticism,* XI (July 1961) *264–73.*

[2] Apparent trisyllables are metrically and probably actually disyllabic. See this chapter, note 13.

[3] See esp. Dedication of the *Aeneid,* Watson, II, *247* (Ker, II, *228–29*).

[4] See Dryden's comment in *Dramatic Poesy,* Watson, I, *21* (Ker, I, *31–32*), but also Dedication of the *Aeneid,* Watson, II, *245* (Ker, II, *226*).

[5] I arrived at the notion "phrase-end" some years ago before I had read any structural linguistics, by noticing that in speech we mark phrase endings even when we do not pause. I have kept the looser term rather than technically discussing the phenomena of juncture and rhythm groups, because my phrase is sufficiently accurate for my purposes. But this is not to dismiss what linguistics can offer the metrist. My understanding of some basic features of meter (in particular, what stress is and is not)

has been clarified for me by linguistics; and there is no doubt that linguistic analysis can refine our technical knowledge of the variations played against metrical schemes. But linguistics refines rather than replaces metrical analysis. Poets such as Dryden who deliberately made iambics knew quite well what they were doing, and the ear remains king. This note is too narrow for a subject that could bear extended comment, and I shall end it by referring to scholars who say some of the crucial things: Seymour Chatman, *Discussions of Poetry: Rhythm and Sound*, ed., George Hemphill (Boston, 1961), *84;* John Thompson, Jr., *The Founding of English Metre* (London, 1961), *1–14, 156;* Harvey Gross, *Sound and Form in Modern Poetry* (Ann Arbor, Mich., 1964), *18–20;* W. K. Wimsatt, Jr. and Monroe Beardsley, *Hateful Contraries* (Lexington, Ky., 1965), *108–45,* esp. *111.* For a concise discussion of "rhythm groups" and "junctures," see Barbara M. H. Strang, *Modern English Structure* (New York, 1965), *56–60.*

⁶ Dryden (Scott), IV, *99* (*The Conquest of Granada*, part I, act V, scene 2).

⁷ Williamson, "Rhetorical Pattern," *78–81.*

⁸ For instance, Sharp, *121–49,* Van Doren, *106.*

⁹ Cp. Earl Miner, *Dryden's Poetry* (Bloomington, Ind., 1967), *84–85,* esp. *84,* "What true nature and true art have in common is . . . truth; what misrepresented nature and witless art have in common is non-sense, unreality."

¹⁰ George Saintsbury, *A History of English Prosody* . . . , 3 vols. (London, 1906–1910), II, *388.*

¹¹ See Van Doren, *261–65,* for a discussion of Dryden's general influence on the romantics. That influence is, I believe, deeper and wider than is usually thought. For a further instance, the end of *The Eve of Saint Agnes* is very like, in diction and theme and tone, the ending of *All for Love*, as is *Ode to a Nightingale*, in several and striking ways, like Dryden's version of *The Flower and the Leaf*.

¹² A sensitive study of the rhetoric and imagery of these famous lines occurs in Rachel Trickett, "The Idiom of Augustan Poetry," *Discussions of Poetry*, ed. Francis Murphy (Boston, 1964), *117–18.*

¹³ In that verse "-ious" and "th' E-" each count as one syllable metrically, whether pronounced as one syllable each (roughly "yus" and "*the*vent") or as one syllable plus a light, metrically uncounted syllable or glide. I strongly suspect the former was Dryden's intent, though proof is hard to come by. I am persuaded, for reasons I state in an unpublished essay, "The Syl-

lables of Shakespeare's Sonnets," that Shakespeare did not intend or use in the sonnets any light, metrically uncounted syllables. The whole matter of metrical "elision" is one of the most vexed and frustrating of problems in poetics.

[14] A similar performance, discussed by Van Doren, *65*, has probably influenced some intense, ghostly lines by Yvor Winters. The cadences are very close. Dryden, *Aeneid*, 5.763–64: "Then in a round the mingl'd Bodies run; / Flying they follow, and pursuing shun." Winters, *Sonnet to the Moon*, vv. 13–14: "Sullen I wait, but still the vision shun. / Bodiless thoughts and thoughtless bodies run." Verses 9–10 of that sonnet are very close in cadence to Dryden's *Amaryllis*, vv. 39–40.

[15] Williamson, "Rhetorical Pattern," *55*.

[16] Dryden (Scott), II, *398* (act I, scene 1).

[17] Dryden (Scott), II, *330* (act III, scene 2).

[18] James Russell Lowell, "Dryden," *Among My Books* (Boston, 1872), *12–14, 29–30, 63–66;* Cecil V. Deane, *Aspects of Eighteenth Century Poetry* (Oxford, 1935), *33–47;* Reuben A. Brower, "Dryden's Poetic Diction and Virgil," *Philological Quarterly*, XVIII (April 1939), *211–17;* Geoffrey Tillotson, "Eighteenth-Century Poetic Diction," *Essays in Criticism and Research* (Cambridge, 1942), *53–85;* John Arthos, *The Language of Natural Description in Eighteenth-Century Poetry* (Ann Arbor, Mich., 1949), *83–86;* Lillian Feder, unpublished Ph.D. dissertation (University of Minnesota, 1951), *87–104;* George Sherburn, "Pope and the 'Great Shew of Nature,'" *The Seventeenth Century* (Stanford, 1951), *306–15;* D. Nichol Smith, *Some Observations on Eighteenth Century Poetry*, 2d ed. (Toronto, 1960), *17–20, 66–70*.

[19] Yvor Winters, *In Defense of Reason* (London, 1960), *134–35*.

6

[1] For instance, as I argue in chapter 8, Dryden's stated view of the form of *All for Love* is a simplification.

[2] *Mirabilis*, Watson, I, *95* (Ker, I, *11*).

[3] Preface to *Absalom and Achitophel*, in *The Poems of John Dryden*, ed. James Kinsley, 4 vols. (Oxford, 1958), I, *216*. Hereafter referred to as Dryden (Kinsley).

[4] Arthur W. Verrall, *Lectures on Dryden*, ed. Margaret de G. Verrall (New York, 1964), *59;* Morris Freedman, "Dryden's Miniature Epic," *Journal of English and German Philology*, LVII (April 1958), *211–19;* A. B. Chambers, "Absalom and Achitophel:

Christ and Satan," *Modern Language Notes*, LXIV (November 1959), *592–96;* Charles E. Ward, *The Life of John Dryden* (Chapel Hill, 1961), *170;* Arthur W. Hoffman, *John Dryden's Imagery* (Gainesville, Fla., 1962), *89*. In virtual prophetic defiance of that phrase, Dryden wrote "Tragedy is the miniature of human life; an epic poem is the draught at length." Dedication of the *Aeneid*, Watson, II, *226* (Ker, II, *157*).

⁵ Dedication of the *Aeneid*, Watson, II, *224* (Ker, II, *155*).

⁶ Preface to *Absalom*, Dryden (Kinsley), I, *216*.

⁷ "Satire," Watson, II, *144–45* (Ker, II, *102*).

⁸ Preface to *Absalom*, Dryden (Kinsley), I, *216*. It is not clear in context whether the image refers to the poem or only to the character of Absalom. But either way it describes the poem. If Absalom's action is incomplete, so is the poem's. *The Medal of John Bayes* (London, 1682) picks up the portrait metaphor for a sneer (Al recto-Al verso): *"We cannot say his* [Dryden's] *Portraiture is done at the full length or has all its Ornaments."* Among critics who use the portrait metaphor are Ruth Wallerstein, "To Madness Near Allied," *Huntington Library Quarterly*, VI (August 1943), *448–49;* Ian Jack, *Augustan Satire* (Oxford, 1952), *73;* Jean H. Hagstrum, *The Sister Arts* (Chicago, 1958), *181;* Hoffman, *90*. The comparison, which probably would not have been offered if the structure had seemed justifiable in more ordinary ways, ignores the action in the poem and the literal invisibility of subject. No poem is ever seen, nor does the composition of a poem exist in the framing of the eye. In poems, the visual, as physically imagined or as analogical, inheres in the sound and meaning, in temporal atemporal structure. Analogies between poems and paintings are interesting, but they mislead. In the present instance, the analogy tends to overrate the importance in the poem of the two groups of characters.

⁹ Watson, II, *149* (Ker, II, *108*). Cp. Chester H. Cable, "Absalom and Achitophel as Epic Satire," *Studies in Honor of John Wilcox*, ed. A. Dayle Wallace and Woodburn O. Ross (Detroit, 1958), *51–60*. I called the poem an "epic satire" in *The Lively and the Just* (Tuscaloosa, Ala., 1962), *40*.

¹⁰ Cp. Earl Miner, *Dryden's Poetry* (Bloomington, Ind., 1967), *134*.

¹¹ The poem's structure has been often criticized, most vehemently by C. S. Lewis in "Shelley, Dryden, and Mr. Eliot," *Rehabilitations* (Oxford, 1939), *8*, and Yvor Winters in *Forms of Discovery* (Denver, 1967), *126*. Lewis is using Dryden polemically to exalt Shelley against Eliot; and Winters, who in his later

career rejected the long poem in general, spares this poem's structure only an inaccurate glance.

[12] Verrall, *54–58;* Hoffman, *72–90,* esp. *82–85;* Bernard Schilling, *Dryden and the Conservative Myth* (New Haven, Conn., 1961), *195–99;* Alan Roper, *Dryden's Poetic Kingdoms* (New York, 1965), *192–98.*

[13] This phrase is discussed skillfully (without application to the poem's structure) by Earl Miner in "Some Characteristics of Dryden's Use of Metaphor," *Dryden,* ed. Bernard Schilling (Englewood Cliffs, N.J., 1963), *117–18.*

[14] And of such Old Testament phrases for God as "the Strength of Israel" (1 Sam. 15:29) and "the Ancient of days" (Dan. 7:9).

[15] Schilling, *Conservative Myth, 309.*

[16] Mary Claire Randolph, "The Structural Design of the Formal Verse Satire," *Essential Articles . . . English Augustan Backgrounds,* ed. Bernard Schilling (Hamden, Conn., 1961), *265.*

[17] Christopher Ricks, in "Dryden's Absalom," *Essays in Criticism,* XI (July 1961), *273–89,* argues that Dryden offers toward Monmouth not "charitable lenience" but "subtle condemnation" (*274*). Dryden evidently offers both, and Ricks is persuasive about some ironic turnings. But Dryden makes abundantly clear that his chief concern with Monmouth was to *"Extenuate, Palliate, and Indulge"* (Preface to *Absalom,* Dryden [Kinsley], I, *216*).

[18] See Kinsley's note to these lines, and John Dryden, *Dryden,* ed. W. D. Christie, 3rd ed. (New York, 1883), note to verse 175 of this poem. Dryden may or may not have known that Shaftesbury was not a party to those negotiations; he surely knew that Charles was formally and factually responsible, more responsible than Shaftesbury could conceivably have been. Charles was king.

[19] Godfrey Davies, *Essays on the Later Stuarts* (San Marino, Calif., 1958), *11–13;* David Ogg, *England in the Reign of Charles II,* 2d ed. (Oxford, 1955), II, *656.*

[20] I am not implying that he did know; that he may have had some notion is at least suggested by the otherwise almost inexplicable verse 87.

[21] That the poem exists, in some loose sense, in a "metaphor," in a comparison of diverse history, is a commonplace truth on which I fear a brilliant scholar, Earl Miner, too heavily relies. In his chapter on this poem, as elsewhere in his book, Miner has much of interest and acuity to say about many things, including metaphors and Dryden's range of metaphorical workings. The

difficulty of his approach is, however, that metaphor becomes so "controlling" it ceases to be metaphor. Metaphor becomes a figure (metaphorically speaking) for almost any development of theme or plot, virtually any discoverable likeness. Any likeness is, of course, an analogy in a broad sense (and any structure requires likenesses), but that does not mean that any likeness is a metaphor in a sense useful to the discussion of literature. Cats are cats because they bear likeness to each other (and to the perceived notion or notions of "cat" amid their variety), but that does not make them metaphorically cats, nor does it make them metaphors for each other. Miner asks, "The problem is to know what to call a metaphor that functions in so many different ways at once" (*92*). It is more of a problem than he manages to dissolve.

The half-hidden thesis of Miner's book is that metaphor is the key to a just understanding of Dryden's poetry. On the face of it, that is false, since metaphor is important but subordinate in Dryden's poetry, since many things besides metaphor are important. The thesis, however, comes to be tautologously true, but only by redefining metaphor until it ceases to have a clear shape or to offer a ground or hope for unity. Critical terms have a tendency to lead us through such dances: "irony" is probably the most famous example in modern criticism. In fact, "metaphor" as Miner uses it comes to mean very nearly the same thing as "irony" as Cleanth Brooks has used it: the power of poems to qualify and refract meanings by context and by various poetic devices.

[22] As is implied by Hoffman, *80–81*.

[23] Verrall, *86–87*.

[24] See George Williamson, "The Restoration Revolt against Enthusiasm," *Studies in Philology*, XXX (October 1933), *571–603*, and Ruth Wallerstein, "To Madness Near Allied," *445–71*.

[25] Jack, *62*.

[26] Verrall, *68–69*.

[27] *Ibid.*, *79–80*. The source, as Kinsley points out in his note to this passage, is Proverbs 30:15–16.

[28] Dryden (Scott), III, *401* (*Tyrannic Love*, act IV, scene 2); Dryden (Scott), V, *243–44* (*Aureng-Zebe*, act IV, scene 1); Dryden (Scott), VII, *440* (*Don Sebastian*, act V, scene 1); *Cinyras and Myrrha*, vv. 39–40. Ovid uses the same sophistry in the original, *Metamorphoses*, x. 324–33.

[29] *To Mr. Lee, on His Alexander*, vv. 33–42.

[30] *To the Memory of Mr. Oldham*, vv. 11–21.

[31] "Parallel," Watson, II, *201* (Ker, II, *145*).

[32] Kinsley's note to these verses.

[33] Louis I. Bredvold, *The Intellectual Milieu of John Dryden* (Ann Arbor, Mich., 1934), *147–48*. See chapter 9, note 5.

[34] Cp. Roper, *17–18*.

[35] Sir John Pollock, *The Popish Plot*, 2d ed. (Cambridge, 1944), *47–69*, esp. *64*. However, George N. Clark, *The Later Stuarts*, 2d ed. (Oxford, 1940) says bluntly "the plot was fictitious" (*88*).

[36] Pollock, *83–166;* Ogg, II, *567–87*.

[37] Ogg, II, *590*.

[38] Dryden was probably remembering a passage from his and Nathaniel Lee's *Oedipus,* Dryden (Scott), VI, *136* (act I, scene 1).

[39] Verrall, *63–64;* Hoffman, *81*.

[40] William Frost, ed., "Introduction," *Selected Works of John Dryden* (New York, 1952), *xvii.*

7

[1] For studies of this genre and its history, see A. W. Verrall, *Lectures on Dryden,* ed. Margaret de G. Verrall (New York, 1964), *176–216;* G. N. Shuster, *The English Ode from Milton to Keats* (New York, 1940), esp. *93–149;* Wallerstein, "On the Death of Mrs. Killigrew," *Articles, 584;* Norman Maclean, "From Action to Image," *Critics and Criticism,* ed. Ronald S. Crane (Chicago, 1952), *408–60;* Paul Ramsey, *The Lively and the Just* (Tuscaloosa, Ala., 1962), *62–98*.

[2] Mark Van Doren, *John Dryden,* 3rd ed. (New York, 1946), *63–64*.

[3] *Davideis,* Book I, in Abraham Cowley, *Poems,* ed. A. R. Waller (Cambridge, 1905), *251*. In his note to this line Cowley solemnly insists that the verse is "so loose, long, and as it were, *Vast* [emphasis his] . . . [in order] to paint in the number the nature of the thing which it describes" (*273*, note 25).

[4] Cp. George Williamson, *The Proper Wit of Poetry* (Chicago, 1961), *133–64;* Earl Miner, *Dryden's Poetry* (Bloomington, Ind., 1967), *267–73*.

[5] Preface to *Tyrannic Love,* Watson, I, *139* (not in Ker).

[6] The following text is quoted from *The Hymnal 1940 Companion* (Protestant Episcopal Church), 2d ed. (New York, 1951), *79*. I do not know what Latin version Dryden used.

Veni, Creator Spiritus,   Accende lumen sensibus,
Mentes tuorum visita,   Infunde amorem cordibus,
Imple superna gratia   Infirma nostra corporis
Quae tu creasti pectora: Virtute firmans perpeti.

Qui Paraclitus diceris,   Hostem repellas longius,
Donum Dei altissimi,   Pacemque dones protinus;
Fons vivus, ignis, caritas,   Ductore sic te praevio
Et spiritalis unctio.   Vitemus omne noxium.

Tu septiformis munere,   Per te sciamus da Patrem,
Dextrae Dei tu digitus,   Noscamus atque Filium,
Tu rite promisso Patris   Te utriusque Spiritum
Sermone ditas guttura.   Credamus omni tempore.

[7] "Satire," Watson, II, *147–48* (Ker, II, *106*).

[8] Saintsbury, *History of English Prosody* . . . , 3 vols. (London, 1906–1910), II, *383*.

[9] Again, as for the songs in chapter 2, I treat this poem more as a poem than as the libretto for a cantata which it, like *Alexander's Feast*, also is. For a close study of its relationship to its first music, see Ernest H. Brennecke, Jr., "Dryden's Ode and Draghi's Music," *PMLA*, XLIX (March 1934), *1–36* (*Articles, 425–65*). Also D. T. Mace, "Musical Humanism, the Doctrine of Rhythmus, and the Saint Cecilia Odes of Dryden," *Journal of the Warburg and Courtauld Institutes*, XXVII (1964), esp. *274*, and R. M. Myers, "Neo-Classical Criticism of the Ode for Music," *PMLA*, LXII (June 1947), *419*. The poem has a substantial overlapping existence as poem and libretto. The overlap is of course considerable; poetic qualities of many sorts can be reflected in music. But the overlap is not entire; when set, every poetic movement gets at least a subtle change of rhythm and timing, and the change may be far from subtle. John Murry Gibbon, *Melody and the Lyric* (New York, 1930), *91–92*, says of Phillip Rosseter's setting of Campion's song "When thou must home to shades of underground," "the musical rhythm does not slavishly follow the verbal rhythm, although they run concurrently." But, when sung, the verbal rhythm becomes not itself but the new shape given it by the setting. For instance, in Rosseter's setting of that poem "When," "thou," "home," "shades," and "of" get equal length, while "un-" and another use of "home" are 1½ times that long. But, if one simply reinforced the iambic rhythm by quantity and isochronism, "When" and "must" would be half as

long as "thou," and "un-" equal in length to "thou." In normal speech and thus in most poetry "un-," a short syllable, would get less quantity than that. The point hardly needs belaboring; poetic values change when set to music. Brennecke says that in *Alexander's Feast* Dryden shows a more flexible grasp of what a libretto should be than he did in the 1687 poem. The examples adduced from the later poem of phrasings which nicely fit vocal polyphony and antiphony are not among the more interesting phrases poetically: "With ravish'd Ears / The Monarch hears" and "Rich the Treasure / Sweet the Pleasure." Brennecke is critical (*29*) of Draghi's opening the last verse of the 1687 poem to "and Musick shall untune the sky, untune, untune, and Musick shall, and Musick shall untune, and Musick shall untune the sky." Whatever the merits of Draghi's music may be, the change ruins the awesome exactitude of the poem's close. One would imagine that the discrepancy in tone and weight between the middle sections of specific imitations (sections 3, 4, 5) and the grandness of the opening and close would pose a problem for the composer as for the critic. Further, there is an oddity of the existence of those sections in relation to the music which would set them. For they are not merely passages which Dryden thought would set well to trumpet, drum, flute, lute and violin. They are distinct, skillful attempts in poetry, in the sound and rhythm of language, to mimic the effects of those instruments. This note carries to (or beyond) the blushing limits of my competency to discuss musical matters, and I shall cease here.

[10] See William Empson's interesting discussion of the rhetoric of the last line of section 3 in *Seven Types of Ambiguity*, 2d ed. (New York, 1947), *198–99*. The effect is perhaps less surprising than Empson finds it. Courage depends on the fears it includes.

[11] D. T. Mace, "Musical Humanism," gives a reason for the discrepancy by showing that the middle sections depend on certain "modern principles of musical thought [namely, Vossius's reading of the concept of *rhythmus,* the power of music to affect emotions directly by meaningful rhythmic structures in words] which were quite inconsistent with and opposed to the principle of older musical thought reflected by the beginning and the end of the poem" (*267*). For further discussion of the older musical theory [*musica mundana, musica humana, musica instrumentalis* as distinguished by Boethius] see, among others, John Hollander, *The Untuning of the Sky* (Princeton, 1961); Gretchen Ludke Finney, *Musical Backgrounds for English Litera-*

ture: 1580–1650 (New Brunswick, N.J., 1961); Leo Spitzer, *Classical and Christian Ideals of World Harmony* (Baltimore, Md., 1962); James Kinsley, "Dryden and the *Encomium Musicae*," *Review of English Studies,* new series, IV (July 1953), *263–67;* Jay Arnold Levine, "Dryden's Song for St. Cecilia's Day," *Philological Quarterly,* XLIV (January 1965), *38–50,* esp. *39–43;* Earl R. Wasserman, "Pope's *Ode for Musick*," *ELH,* XXVIII (June 1961), *163–86,* esp. *166–69.*

[12] Verrall, *194.*

[13] Cp. Lucretius, *De Rerum Natura,* ed. Cyril Bailey (Oxford, 1947), book I, vv. 159–214 (vol. I, *184–87*) and note (vol. II, *626–28*) and introduction, I, *58–60; Selections from Early Greek Philosophy,* ed. Milton C. Nahm, 3rd ed. (New York, 1947), *68–74;* A. E. Taylor, *Plato,* 6th ed. (London, 1949), *124* and note, pp. *444–47,* as well as works cited in note 11 of this chapter. Miner, *Dryden's Poetry, 274–88,* esp. *284–85,* discusses various intellectual traditions drawn on and to some degree "harmonized" in the poem.

[14] Cp. Levine, "Dryden's Song," *41.*

[15] Cp. Hollander, *408–409.*

[16] Verrall, *194–95.* Wasserman, "Pope's *Ode*," *166–67,* argues that Verrall's view is incorrect since the section, as a whole, has a comprehensible stanzaic pattern. Wasserman does not count "high" as a rhyme with "harmony," hence comes up with a different and neater pattern than the one I describe. Levine, "Dryden's Song," *38–39* has the same pattern as I. To rhyme "high" and "harmony" is common enough in the period, but either pattern suggests the powerful impact of the struggle to composing, the *discordia concors,* the "rivalry" (cp. Wasserman, "Pope's *Ode*," *164–65*) between chaos and order in the section. Dryden ends the section with a heroic couplet, arriving home to the form most powerfully congenial to his mastering touch.

[17] Levine, "Dryden's Song," *43.*

[18] As quoted by Finney, *x.*

[19] Finney, *x–xi,* describes Raphael's "Ecstasy of Saint Cecilia," in which St. Cecilia, "portable organ in hand, viol at her feet, gazes raptly at a choir of angels." Cp. Jean Hagstrum, *The Sister Arts* (Chicago, 1958), *203–205,* and plate XII (the painting by Raphael) and plate XIII, Orazio Gentileschi, "Saints Valerian, Tiburtus and Cecilia." Such paintings represent, Hagstrum says, a widespread tradition. There is, however, a neat if accidental kinship between the two paintings and Dryden's poem. In Raphael's painting the focus is to the "Choires above," as in section

VI of the poem. In Gentileschi's painting the angel is coming down, as in Dryden's section VII.

[20] Miner, *Dryden's Poetry*, 273–74, remarks the "greater personal intensity" occasioned by Dryden's conversion in this poem, *The Hind and the Panther*, and the Anne Killigrew Ode. Cp. my discussion of the Anne Killigrew Ode, *Lively*, 66.

[21] See Helge Kökeritz, *Shakespeare's Pronunciation* (New Haven, Conn., 1953), 388.

8

[1] The imagery is richly and perceptively discussed by Earl Miner, *Dryden's Poetry* (Bloomington, Ind., 1967), 36–73, esp. 42–44, 50–53. For reasons I hope I make clear in this chapter and in chapter 6, note 21, I cannot accept Miner's view of the primacy (or virtual primacy) of imagery in the structure of the play.

[2] I use similar notation throughout this chapter, referring to the text of the play in John Dryden, *John Dryden: Four Tragedies*, ed. L. A. Beaurline and Fredson Bowers (Chicago, 1967), 209–280. Each act contains only one scene, hence no scene references are needed. The symbols a and b after numbers refer to the first and last part respectively of a line divided between two speakers.

[3] Miner, *Dryden's Poetry*, 45, calls the same passage "a static dance."

[4] John Churton Collins, *Essays and Studies* (London, 1895), 36–37; George Saintsbury, *Dryden* (New York, 1895), 58–59; Adolphus W. Ward, *A History of English Dramatic Literature* (London, 1899), II, 372–73; Ashley H. Thorndike, *Tragedy* (Boston, 1908), 260–61; George Henry Nettleton, *English Drama of the Restoration and Eighteenth Century* (New York, 1914), 90–91; Margaret Sherwood, *Dryden's Dramatic Theory and Practice* (New Haven, Conn., 1914), 85–88; Allardyce Nicoll, *British Drama* (New York, 1925), 234–35; Bonamy Dobrée, *Restoration Tragedy* (Oxford, 1929), 75–76; David Nichol Smith, *John Dryden* (Hamden, Conn., 1966), 40–43; Kenneth Young, *John Dryden* (London, 1954), 100–102. Selma Assir Zebouni, *Dryden* (Baton Rouge, La., 1965), 51–54, derogates the plot, finding the play rankly sentimental (cp. this chapter, note 6). I agree that most of the passages

cited by Zebouni are flawed by sentimentality; but I would strongly deny that such passages are frequent or typical.

[5] 1.47 for "dream" and 1.206–209 for passives and metaphor.

[6] A notion encouraged by the wit of the prologue to the play, vv. 10–15. Arthur C. Kirsch, *Dryden's Heroic Drama* (Princeton, N.J., 1965), who twice quotes from the prologue (Kirsch, *128*, *132*), finds that the play is "essentially" sentimental rather than active (*132*).

[7] See Dryden (Scott), V, *291*; Nicoll, *234–35*; Thorndike, *260–61*; F. R. Leavis, " 'Antony and Cleopatra' and 'All for Love,' " *Scrutiny*, V (September 1936), *167*. For a different view, see R. J. Kaufman, "On the Poetics of Terminal Tragedy," *Dryden*, ed. Bernard Schilling (Englewood Cliffs, N.J., 1963), *93*.

[8] William Archer, *The Old Drama and the New* (Boston, 1923), *151*.

[9] For instance, Sherwood, *88–89*; Leavis, *167*; Moody E. Prior, "Tragedy and the Heroic Play," *Dryden*, ed. Schilling, *97*; Miner, *Dryden's Poetry*, *58*.

[10] Cp. Miner, *Dryden's Poetry*, *56*, on "the pretense on all sides."

[11] An inconsistency also noted by Miner, *Dryden's Poetry*, *39–40*; Bruce King, *Dryden's Major Plays* (New York, 1966), *140–41*; and Beaurline and Bowers, *193*.

[12] Watson, I, *222* (Ker, I, *191*).

[13] See Prior, *Dryden*, ed. Schilling, *95–114*, esp. *95–98*.

[14] I am not suggesting that this morality is the exclusive morality of the other plays. For a major change, and softening, in *Aureng-Zebe* and later plays, see Kirsch, esp. *118–28*.

[15] "Gaudy" is to Dryden a full pun, sharing the jostling meanings of "joyous" (from latin *gaudere*) and "showy." Cp. *Absalom and Achitophel*, v. 297, "Not barren Praise alone, that Gaudy Flower." The OED shows both meanings in the seventeenth century. Dryden elsewhere uses the word in its wholly laudatory meaning: for example, *The Flower and the Leaf*, v. 106.

[16] Cp. W. K. Wimsatt, Jr., *The Verbal Icon* (Lexington, Ky., 1954), *181*, a witty exposition of metrical wit.

[17] Leavis, *165*.

[18] As Neander calls repartee in *An Essay of Dramatic Poesy*, Watson, I, *60* (Ker, I, 72).

[19] A verse which borrows directly from *Much Ado About Nothing*, act III, scene 2, verses 109 and 110 (Neilson-Hill text and numbering). "Cleopatra" offers a richer rhythm than "Hero."

[20] Ruth Wallerstein, "Dryden and the Analysis of Shakespeare's Techniques," *Articles, 563.*

9

[1] As even Kinsley has to admit in his well argued defense of Dryden's habits of praise, James Kinsley, "Dryden and the Art of Praise," *English Studies,* XXXIV (April 1953), *57–64 (Articles, 541–50).*

[2] The Muse's flight of verses 850–55, which is valuable structurally.

[3] Even David Nichol Smith, in his laudatory and sensitive *John Dryden* (Cambridge, 1950) ends on the note of "force, ease, . . . vigour" (*90*). Surely. But there are higher and as true notes of praise.

[4] Samuel Johnson, *Lives of the English Poets,* ed. G. B. Hill, 3 vols. (Oxford, 1905), I, *464–65.*

[5] Bredvold's study (see chapter 6, note 33), valuable as it is in tracing the Pyrrhonistic tradition in the seventeenth century, a tradition into which Dryden dipped on a few occasions for arguments, considerably overrates Dryden's dependence on that tradition and the "sceptical" nature of his mind. See Hoyt Trowbridge, "The Place of Rules in Dryden's Criticism," *Modern Philology,* XLIV (November 1946); Edward N. Hooker, "Dryden and the Atoms of Epicurus," *ELH,* XXIV (September 1957), *177–90 (Articles, 232–44)*; Elias J. Chiasson, "Dryden's Apparent Scepticism in *Religio Laici,*" *Harvard Theological Review,* LIV (July 1961), *207–21 (Articles, 245–60)*; Thomas H. Fujimari, "Dryden's *Religio Laici,*" *PMLA,* LXXVI (June 1961), *205–17*; Bruce King, "The Significance of Dryden's *State of Innocence,*" *Studies in English Literature,* IV (Summer 1964), *371–91*; Victor M. Hamm, "Dryden's *Religio Laici* and Roman Catholic Apologetics," *PMLA,* LXXX (June 1965), *190–98.*

[6] Cp. Earl Miner, "Some Characteristics of Dryden's Use of Metaphor," *Dryden,* ed. Bernard Schilling (Englewood Cliffs, N.J., 1963), *116.*

[7] My discussion is of the 1922 essay in T. S. Eliot, "John Dryden," *Selected Essays* (New York, 1932), *264–74,* rather than the three collected essays *John Dryden* (New York, 1932). The latter work offers some praise which is even flatter in tone. "I can think of no name in literature whose aims are so exactly

fulfilled by his performance, and in the whole vineyard no labourer who more deserved his hire" (*23*).

[8] Mark Van Doren, *John Dryden*, 3rd ed. (New York, 1946), *vii.*

[9] *Ibid., vii.*

[10] *Ibid.,* esp. *38–41.*

[11] *The Medal of John Bayes* (London, 1682) admits *that* much: "In Verse, thou hast a knack with words to chime, / And had'st a kind of Excellence in Rime" (*4*).

[12] Respectively:

1. Dryden (Scott), III, *395* (*Tyrannic Love,* act IV, scene 1).
2. Dryden (Scott), III, *425* (*Tyrannic Love,* act V, scene 1).
3. *Theodore and Honoria,* vv. 62–63.
4. Prologue to *His Royal Highness,* vv. 5–6.
5. *All for Love,* 2.205–206.
6. *Threnodia Augustalis,* vv. 63–66.
7. Dryden (Scott), VI, *407* (*The Spanish Friar,* act II, scene 1).
8. Dryden (Scott), V, *159* (*The State of Innocence,* act V, scene 1).
9. Dryden (Scott), VI, *355* (*Troilus and Cressida,* act V, scene 2).
10. *To the Dutchess of Ormond,* vv. 151–52.
11. *The Hind and the Panther,* part I, vv. 1–4.
12. *To the Memory of Mr. Oldham,* vv. 19–21.
13. *To the Pious Memory of Mistress Anne Killigrew,* vv. 191–92.

[13] Cp. George McFadden, "Dryden and the Numbers of His Native Tongue," *Essays and Studies in Language and Literature,* ed. Herbert H. Petit (Pittsburgh, 1964), *108.*

[14] The distinction is, let me hope, not totally lunatic. Marlowe may well be a greater playwright than Jonson; he is hardly a better playwright than Jonson.

[15] William Congreve, "Preface to Dryden's Dramatic Works," *The Complete Works of William Congreve,* ed. Montague Summers, 4 vols. (London, 1923), IV, *179–85.*

Index of Names

Ainger, Alfred, 191n2
Archer, William, 147
Aristotle, 3, 6, 11, 99, 150–51
Arnold, Matthew, 169, 170, 178–79

Baker, Herschel, 185n3
Boethius, 139
Boileau, Nicolas, 96
Bossu, 10, 11, 12
Bredvold, Louis I., 116, 169, 170, 180, 206n5
Brennecke, Ernest, 201n9
Brooks, Cleanth, 186n11, 187n12, 198n21
Browne, William, 26, 30
Bush, Douglas, 185n3
Butler, Samuel, 21, 130
Butterfield, Herbert, 194n21

Campion, Thomas, 26, 31–32, 201n9
Charles I, king of England, 54–55
Charles II, king of England, 67, 97–101, 103–108, 110–20, 198n18
Chaucer, Geoffrey, 14, 31, 85–89, 168, 173, 178
Coleridge, Samuel Taylor, 55, 178–79
Congreve, William, 31, 181
Cowley, Abraham, 61, 126–27, 200n3
Crane, Ronald S., 186n11, 187n12
Croce, Benedetto, 187n12
Cromwell, Oliver, 52–63, 192n5

Davenant, Sir William, 53
Donne, John, 27, 31, 61, 173, 178

DRYDEN, JOHN:
—Criticism: "The Author's Apology for Heroic Poetry," 3–4, 6, 7, 9; Dedication of the *Aeneid*, 15, 18, 69–70, 96; Dedication of *The Rival Ladies*, 1; Dedication of *The Spanish Friar*, 6; "A Defence of An Essay of Dramatic Poesy," 2, 3, 12, 157; "A Discourse Concerning Satire," 1, 9–10, 12, 33, 96–97, 130, 188n28; "An Essay of Dramatic Poesy," 2, 6, 7, 12–13, 13–14, 16, 60–61, 70, 94, 159, 170, 176–77, 186n11; "The Life of Lucian," 6; "A Parallel betwixt Painting and Poetry," 7, 10, 114; Postscript to the *Aeneid*, 14; Preface to *Absalom and Achitophel*, 95–96, 198n17; Preface to *Albion and Albanius*, 6, 15; Preface to *All for Love*, 145, 149–52; Preface to *Annus Mirabilis*, 6, 9, 15, 16, 18–19, 52; Preface to *Eleonora*, 9; Preface to *An Evening's Love*, 7–8; Preface to the *Fables*, 9, 31, 170; Preface to *Sylvae*, 5, 6, 9, 15, 16, 17, 18; Preface to *Troilus and Cressida*, 5–6, 10–11, 13; Preface to *Tyrannic Love*, 16, 128–29; *Prosodia*, 15
—Poems and plays: *Absalom and Achitophel*, 12, 22–23, 27, 56, 67, 71–72, 93, 94, 95–125, 168, 170, 173, 181, 205n15; *Absalom and Achitophel*, the second part, 26; *Aeneid* (tr),

209

Index of Subjects